Read *With* Me

A Story Bible for

D0120257

Presented to: ISABEL ROBINSON

By: CRAIG AND JESSICA

On: CHRISTMAS 2001

Read *With* Me Bible

A Story Bible for Children

ILLUSTRATED BY

Dennis Jones

EDITED BY

Doris Rikkers and Jean E. Syswerda

**CANDLE
BOOKS**

ISBN 1 85985 190 8
Published in the UK by Candle Books 1998,
Reprinted 1999, 2000, 2001
Distributed by STL
PO Box 300, Carlisle, CA3 0QS

Worldwide coedition organised and produced by
Angus Hudson Ltd, Concorde House, Grenville Place,
Mill Hill, London NW7 3SA, England
Tel: +44 20 8959 3668 Fax: +44 20 8959 3678

Printed in Singapore

Contents

OLD TESTAMENT

NEW TESTAMENT

OLD
TESTAMENT

God Creates the World
Genesis 1

In the beginning God created
the heavens and the earth.
God said, "Let there be light."
And there was light.

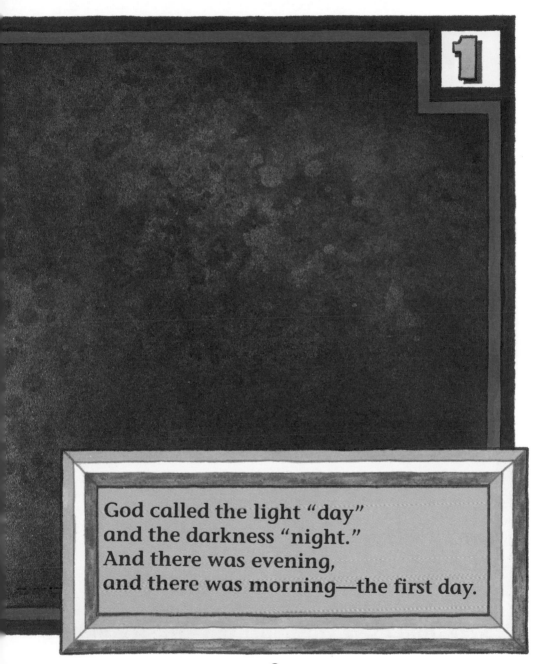

God called the light "day"
and the darkness "night."
And there was evening,
and there was morning—the first day.

God said, "Let there be space
between the waters."
God called the space "sky."
And there was evening,
and there was morning—the second day.

God said, "Let dry ground appear."
Then God said, "Let the land
grow plants and trees."
And there was evening,
and there was morning—the third day.

God said, "Let there
be lights in the sky."
God made two great lights.
The greater light for the day
and the lesser light for the night.
He also made the stars.
And there was evening,
and there was morning—the fourth day.

6

God said, "Let the water
be full of living creatures.
Let birds fly in the sky."
And there was evening,
and there was morning—the fifth day.

God said, "Let the land
produce living creatures."
And it was so. Then God said,
"Let us make man in our image."
So God created man in his own image.

God saw all that he had made,
and it was very good.
And there was evening,
and there was morning—the sixth day.
On the seventh day God rested.

The Garden of Eden

Genesis 2

God planted a garden in Eden.
He made all kinds of trees grow—
trees that were pretty to look at
and good for food.
In the middle of the garden
were the tree of life and the tree
of the knowledge of good and evil.

God put Adam in the Garden of Eden
to take care of it.
God brought all the animals
and all the birds to Adam
to see what he would name them.
So Adam gave names to all
of the animals and birds.

And God said, "You are free to eat
from any tree in the garden.
But you must not eat from the tree
of the knowledge of good and evil.
If you eat of it, you will die."

Adam and Eve

Genesis 2

God said, "It is not good
for the man to be alone.
I will make a helper for him."
So God made Adam fall asleep.
He took one of Adam's ribs
and made a woman from it.
Adam named his wife Eve.

Adam and Eve Disobey God

Genesis 3

The snake was more crafty
than any of the wild animals.
He said to Eve, "Did God really say that you
must not eat from any tree in the garden?"
Eve said, "We may eat fruit
from the trees in the garden.

But we must not eat fruit from the tree in the middle of the garden.
We must not touch it, or we will die."
"You will not die," the snake said.
"God knows that when you eat the fruit your eyes will be opened.
You will be like God."

Eve took some fruit and ate it.
She also gave some to Adam, and he ate it.

Then they realized they were naked.
So they sewed fig leaves together
and covered themselves.
And they hid from God.

In the cool of the day
God called Adam, "Where are you?"
Adam answered, "I heard you, and I was
afraid because I was naked. So I hid."
God said, "Who told you that you were naked?
Have you eaten from the tree
that I told you not to eat from?"

Adam said, "Eve gave me some fruit,
and I ate it."
Then God said to Eve, "What have you done?"
Eve said, "The serpent tricked me, and I ate."
So God sent Adam and Eve away
from the Garden of Eden.

Cain and Abel

Genesis 4

Eve gave birth to Cain and Abel.
Now Abel kept flocks.
Cain worked the soil.

One day Cain and Abel
brought an offering to God.
God liked Abel and his offering.
But Cain and his offering did not please God.
So Cain was very angry.

Cain said to his brother Abel,
"Let's go out to the field."
While they were in the field,
Cain killed Abel.

Then God said to Cain,
"What have you done?
Where is your brother Abel?"
"I don't know," he replied.
"Am I my brother's keeper?"
So Cain left God's presence
and lived in the land of Nod.

The Flood and Noah's Ark

Genesis 6–7

Noah was a righteous man,
and he walked with God.

Now the earth was very sinful in God's sight.
So God said to Noah, "Make yourself an ark.
I am going to bring a flood to destroy
every creature that is alive.

Bring into the ark two of all living creatures, male and female. Take food to eat and store it away for you and for them."

Noah did everything just as God commanded him.

Noah and his family entered the ark.
The waters rose and the ark floated.
Every living thing on the face
of the earth was wiped out.

Only Noah was left,
and those with him in the ark.

God's Promise to Noah

Genesis 7–8

The waters flooded the earth for 150 days.
But God remembered Noah
and all the animals in the ark.
God sent a wind over the earth,
and the water went away.
The ark came to rest on a mountain.

After 40 days Noah opened the window.

Noah sent out a raven.
It kept flying back and forth.

Then Noah sent out a dove.

 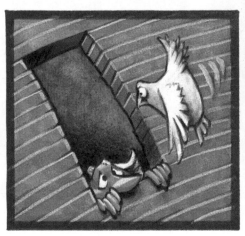

The dove could find no place to land
because of all the water.

So it returned to Noah.

Noah waited seven more days
and again sent out the dove.
When the dove returned,
in its beak was a fresh olive leaf!
Noah waited seven more days
and sent the dove out again.
This time it did not return.

So Noah, his family, and all the animals
and birds came out of the ark.
God said to Noah and his sons,
"Never again will I destroy
all living creatures.

As long as the earth lasts,
seedtime and harvest,
cold and heat, summer and winter,
day and night will never cease.
I have set my rainbow in the clouds.
It will be the sign of the promise
between me and the earth."

The Tower of Babel

Genesis 11

Now the whole world spoke one language.
The men said to each other,
"Let's build a city,
with a tower that reaches heaven.

Let's make a name for ourselves
and not be scattered over the earth."

But God came down to see the city
and the tower the men were building.
He said, "If by speaking
the same language they can do this,
then nothing will be impossible for them.
I will confuse their language
so they will not understand each other."

So God scattered the people
all over the earth.
They stopped building the city.
That is why it was called Babel—
because there God confused
the language of the whole world.

God's Promises to Abraham

Genesis 12; 15; 17

God said to Abraham, "Leave your country, your people and your father's household.
Go to the land I will show you.
I will make you into a great nation, and I will bless you.
I will make your name great."

Abraham was 75 years old
when he left his home.
He took his wife Sarah, his nephew Lot,
and all their possessions and people.
They set out for the land of Canaan.

When Abraham was 99 years old,
God appeared to him and said,
"Walk with me and do what is right.
You will be the father of many nations.
Look up at the heavens and count the stars.

That's how many children you will have."
God also said to Abraham, "As for Sarah, your
wife, I will bless her and give her a son,
and you will call him Isaac."

Abraham Offers Isaac to God

Genesis 21–22

God was gracious to Sarah.
He did what he promised, and Sarah had a son.
Abraham named his son Isaac.

Some time later God tested Abraham.
He said to him, "Abraham! Take your only son,
Isaac, whom you love, and go to Moriah.
Sacrifice him there as a burnt offering."

Early the next morning Abraham got up
and saddled his donkey.
When he had cut enough wood for the offering,
he and Isaac set out. Abraham took the wood
for the burnt offering and gave it to Isaac to carry.
He carried the fire and the knife.

As they walked, Isaac said, "Father, the fire and wood are here, but where is the lamb for the burnt offering?" Abraham answered, "God will provide the lamb, my son."

Abraham built an altar and put the wood on it. He tied up his son Isaac and laid him on the altar. Then he took the knife to kill his son.

But an angel called out to him from heaven,
"Abraham! Abraham! Do not lay a hand on the boy.
Now I know that you love God, because you have
not withheld from me your son, your only son."
Abraham looked up.
There in a bush he saw a ram caught by its horns.
So he sacrificed the ram instead of his son.

Isaac and Rebekah

Genesis 24

Abraham said to his servant, "Go to my country and my relatives and get a wife for my son Isaac." Then the servant took ten camels and made his way to the town of Nahor.

The camels knelt down
near the well outside the town.
It was towards evening,
the time the women go out to draw water.

Then the servant prayed, "O God
of my master Abraham, when I say to a girl,
'Please let down your jar and give me a drink,'
and she says, 'Drink, and I'll water
your camels too'—let her be the one
you have chosen for Isaac."

Before he had finished praying,
Rebekah came out with her jar on her shoulder.
She was very beautiful.
The servant hurried to meet her and said,
"Please give me a little water from your jar."
After she had given him a drink, she said,
"I'll draw water for your camels too."

When the camels had finished drinking,
the servant gave Rebekah
a gold nose ring and two gold bracelets.

Rebekah's brother Laban hurried out to the spring.
The servant told him about his prayer.
Laban said, "This is from God."
So they asked Rebekah,
"Will you go with this man?"
"I will go," she said.
So Rebekah became Isaac's wife.
And he loved her.

Esau and Jacob

Genesis 25

Isaac prayed to God for his wife Rebekah
because she didn't have any children.
God answered Isaac's prayer,
and Rebekah had twin boys, Esau and Jacob.

The boys grew up.
Esau became a hunter, but Jacob was a quiet man.
Isaac, who had a taste for wild game, loved Esau.
But Rebekah loved Jacob.

Once Jacob was cooking some stew
when Esau came in from the country.
Esau was starving. He said to Jacob,
"Quick, let me have some of that red stew!
I'm starving!"
Jacob replied, "First sell me your birthright."
"Look, I'm about to die," Esau said.
"What good is the birthright to me?"
So Esau sold his birthright to Jacob.

Then Jacob gave Esau some bread and some stew, and he ate and drank.
So Esau despised his birthright.

Jacob Gets Isaac's Blessing

Genesis 27

When Isaac was old
he could no longer see. He called for Esau and
said to him, "I am now an old man.
Bring me some wild game to eat,
so that I may give you my blessing before I die."

Now Rebekah was listening.

When Esau left, Rebekah said to Jacob,
"Listen carefully and do what I tell you.
Bring me two young goats.
I will prepare some tasty food.
You take it to your father to eat,
so that he may give you his blessing."

Jacob said to his mother,
"But my brother Esau is a hairy man,
and I'm a man with smooth skin.
What if my father touches me?"
His mother said, "Just do what I say."
Then she took the best clothes of Esau and
put them on Jacob. She covered his hands
and his neck with goatskins.

Then she handed Jacob the food
and the bread she had made.
Jacob went to his father and said,
"I am Esau your firstborn."
Jacob went close to Isaac, who touched him
and said, "The voice is the voice of Jacob,
but the hands are the hands of Esau."

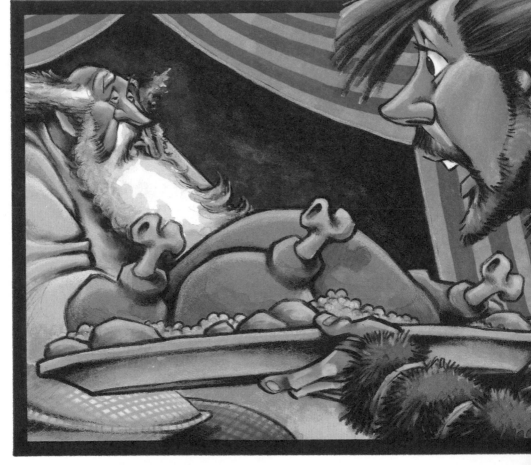

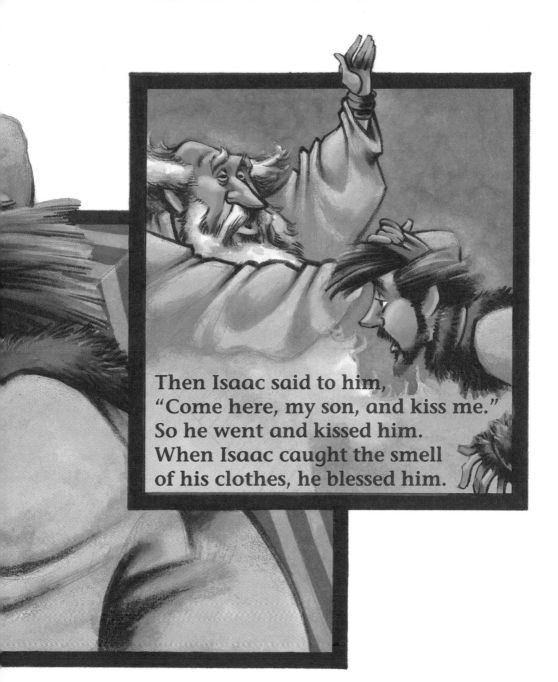

Then Isaac said to him,
"Come here, my son, and kiss me."
So he went and kissed him.
When Isaac caught the smell
of his clothes, he blessed him.

Esau held a grudge against Jacob because of the blessing his father had given him.

Jacob's Dream at Bethel

Genesis 28

Jacob left home.
He stopped for the night because the sun had set.
He put a stone under his head
and lay down to sleep.

Jacob had a dream.
He saw a stairway resting on the earth,
with its top reaching to heaven.
The angels were going up and down on it.
God stood at the top and said:
"I am the Lord. I will give you and
your children this land. I am with you.
I will watch over you wherever you go."

Jacob Marries Leah and Rachel

Genesis 29–30

Jacob's uncle Laban had two daughters,
Leah and Rachel.

Jacob was in love with Rachel.
He said to Laban, "I'll work for you
seven years for your younger daughter Rachel."
Laban said, "I'll give her to you."
So Jacob served seven years to get Rachel.
But the years seemed like only a few days
to him because he loved her so much.

Laban gave a feast for the wedding.
But he took his daughter Leah
and gave her to Jacob, instead of Rachel.
When morning came, there was Leah!
Jacob said to Laban, "What have you done?
Why have you tricked me?"

Laban replied, "It is not our custom to give the younger daughter in marriage before the older one. I will give you Rachel too if you work for me another seven years." So Jacob had two wives.
But he loved Rachel more than Leah.

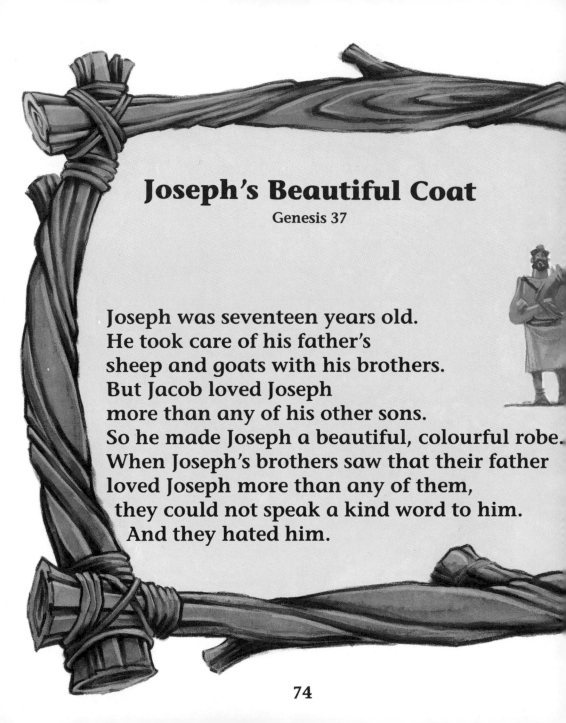

Joseph's Beautiful Coat

Genesis 37

Joseph was seventeen years old.
He took care of his father's
sheep and goats with his brothers.
But Jacob loved Joseph
more than any of his other sons.
So he made Joseph a beautiful, colourful robe.
When Joseph's brothers saw that their father
loved Joseph more than any of them,
they could not speak a kind word to him.
And they hated him.

Joseph's Dreams

Genesis 37

Joseph had a dream. He said to his brothers, "Listen to this dream I had. We were binding sheaves of grain out in the field. Suddenly my sheaf rose and your sheaves gathered around mine and bowed down." His brothers said to him, "Will you actually rule us?" And they hated him because of his dream.

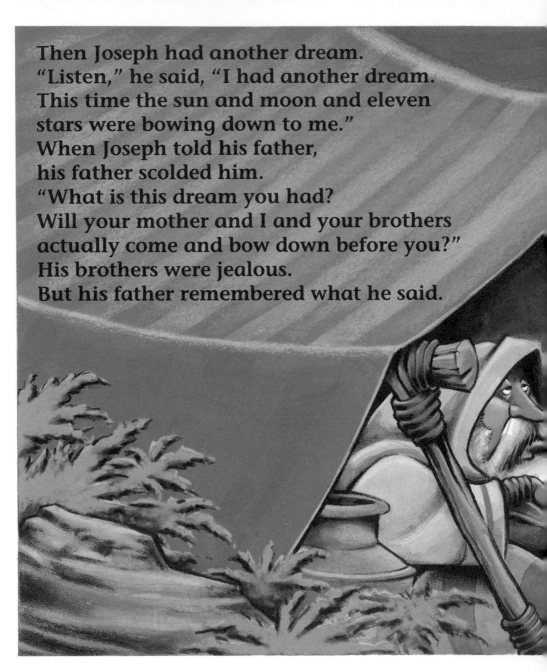

Then Joseph had another dream.
"Listen," he said, "I had another dream.
This time the sun and moon and eleven
stars were bowing down to me."
When Joseph told his father,
his father scolded him.
"What is this dream you had?
Will your mother and I and your brothers
actually come and bow down before you?"
His brothers were jealous.
But his father remembered what he said.

Joseph Sold Into Slavery

Genesis 37

Joseph's brothers were feeding
their father's flocks near Shechem.
Jacob said to Joseph, "Go and see if all is well
with your brothers and with the flocks."
So Joseph went after his brothers.

But they saw him in the distance.
Before he reached them, they planned to kill him.
"Here comes that dreamer!" they said.
"Let's kill him.
We'll say that a wild animal ate him."

When Reuben heard this, he tried to rescue Joseph.
"Let's not kill him," he said.
"Let's just throw him into the well."
When Joseph came, the brothers took his
beautiful robe and threw him into the well.
Judah said to his brothers,
"Let's sell Joseph. Let's not kill him.
After all, he is our brother."

When a camel caravan came by,
the brothers sold Joseph to the camel drivers,
who took him to Egypt.
Then the brothers got Joseph's robe.
They killed a goat and dipped the robe in the blood

They took the robe back to their father
and said, "We found this."
Jacob said, "It's my son's robe!
Some wild animal has eaten him!"
Jacob was very sad. He cried for many days.

Meanwhile, the camel drivers sold Joseph in Egypt to a man named Potiphar.

Joseph's Brothers Go to Egypt

Genesis 42; 45; 47

Throughout the world there was no food to eat.
When Jacob learned that there was grain
in Egypt, he said to his sons,
"Go and buy some for us, so that we will not die."
Ten of Joseph's brothers went to Egypt to buy grain.

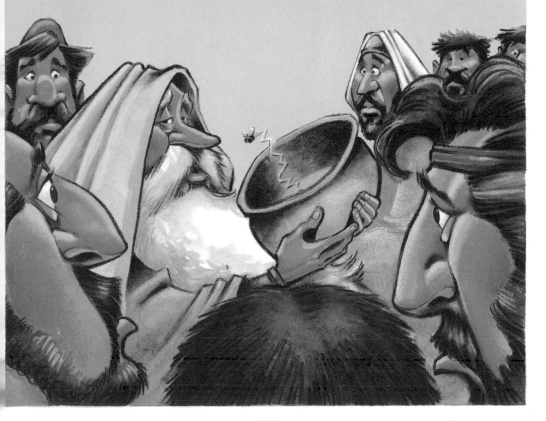

Now Joseph was the governor of the land.
He sold grain to all the people.
So when Joseph's brothers arrived,
they bowed down to Joseph.
As soon as Joseph saw his brothers,
he recognized them.

But he pretended to be a stranger.
He spoke harshly to them. "You are spies!"
"No, my lord," they answered.
"Your servants have come to buy food.
We are honest men, not spies."

Then Joseph could no longer control himself,
and he cried out, "I am Joseph!
Is my father still living?"
But his brothers were not able
to answer him. They were terrified.
Then Joseph said to his brothers,
"Come close to me. I am your brother Joseph,
the one you sold into Egypt!
Don't be angry with yourselves for selling me.
God sent me ahead of you to save your lives."

So Joseph settled his father
and his brothers in Egypt.
He gave them property
in the best part
of the land.

The Israelites Made Slaves in Egypt

Exodus 1

Joseph and all his brothers died.
But the Israelites had many, many children.

A new king came to power in Egypt.
"Look," he said to his people,
"there are too many Israelites.
If war breaks out, they will join
our enemies and fight against us."

So they put slave masters over them.
They made their lives bitter with hard work.
Then Pharaoh gave this order:
"Every Hebrew boy that is born
you must throw into the Nile River.
But let every girl live."

Pharaoh's Daughter Finds Moses

Exodus 2

An Israelite woman gave birth to a son.
When she saw that he was a healthy child,
she hid him for three months.

But when she couldn't hide him any longer,
she placed the child in a basket
and put it among the reeds near the Nile River.
The baby's sister, Miriam, stood at a distance
to see what would happen to him.

Pharaoh's daughter went down
to the Nile to take a bath.
She saw the basket among the reeds
and sent her slave girl to get it.
She opened the basket and saw the baby.
He was crying, and she felt sorry for him.
"This is one of the Hebrew babies," she said.

Then Miriam asked Pharaoh's daughter,
"Should I go and get one of the Hebrew
women to nurse the baby for you?"
"Yes, go," she answered.
And the girl got the baby's mother.

So the woman took the baby and nursed him.
When the child grew older,
she took him to Pharaoh's daughter.
He became her son, and she named him Moses.

Moses and the Burning Bush

Exodus 3–4

One day Moses was watching sheep in the desert.
Moses saw a bush that was on fire,
but it didn't burn up.

God called to Moses from within the bush,
"Moses! Moses!"
And Moses said, "Here I am."
"Don't come any closer," God said.
"Take off your sandals.
You are standing on holy ground."

Then God said, "I have seen the misery of my people in Egypt. I have heard them crying. I know they are suffering.
I have come down to rescue them. So now, go. Tell Pharaoh to let my people go."
So Moses took his wife and sons and started back to Egypt.

The First Five Plagues

Exodus 5–9

Moses and his brother Aaron went to Pharaoh and said, "Let my people go so they can worship God in the desert or he may send plagues." Pharaoh said, "I don't know your God. And I will not let your people go."

105

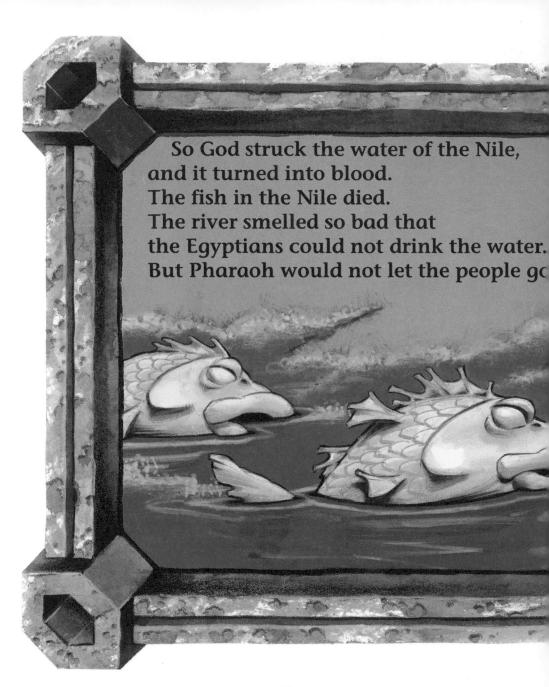

So God struck the water of the Nile,
and it turned into blood.
The fish in the Nile died.
The river smelled so bad that
the Egyptians could not drink the water.
But Pharaoh would not let the people go

Then Moses said to Pharaoh,
"Let my people go." Pharaoh said, "No!"
So God sent frogs to cover the land.
The frogs came into the palace
and jumped on the beds.

They came into the kitchens and filled the ovens.
Pharaoh said to Moses, "Pray to your God to take
these frogs away, and I will let your people go."
Moses did. The frogs died.
But Pharaoh would not let the people go.

Then Moses said to Pharaoh,
"Let my people go." And Pharaoh said, "No!"
So God turned the dust of Egypt into gnats.
There were gnats on all the people
and on every animal. But Pharaoh was stubborn
and would not let the people go.

So God sent swarms of flies.
The flies covered the people and the ground.
They poured into the palace.
Pharaoh called to Moses, "Pray to your God
to take these flies away.
Then I will let your people go."
Moses did. The flies disappeared.
But Pharaoh would not let the people go.

Then Moses said, "Let my people go."
Pharaoh said, "No!"
So God sent a terrible plague on all the animals.
The horses, the donkeys, the camels,
the sheep and the goats all died.
But Pharaoh would not let the people go.

Four More Plagues

Exodus 9–12

Moses tossed some ashes into the air.
God turned the ashes into a fine dust
that made sores break out
on all the people and the animals.
But Pharaoh did nothing.

So God sent thunder and hail.
Hail beat down everything growing in the fields.
It stripped every tree.
Pharaoh said to Moses, "I've been wrong.
You are right. Pray to your God to stop
the thunder and hail."
Moses did. The thunder and hail stopped.
But Pharaoh would not let the people go.

So God sent swarms of locusts.
They covered the ground until it was black.
They ate all that was left after the hail.
Nothing green was left. Pharaoh said to Moses,
"Pray to your God to take these locusts away.
Then I will let your people go."
Moses did. The locusts flew away.
But Pharaoh would not let the people go.

Then Moses pointed to the sky.
Darkness covered Egypt for three days.
No one could see anyone else.
Pharaoh called Moses, "Go, worship your God.
But leave your flocks and herds behind."
Moses said, "Our animals must go with us."
So Pharaoh would not let the people go.
God said to Moses, "I will send one more plague.
After that, Pharaoh will let you go."

The Last Plague

Exodus 12

Moses said to the elders of Israel, "Each man is to take a lamb for his family. The animal must be one year old.

Kill the lambs at sunset.
Put some of the blood on the top and
on both sides of the door of your house.
When God goes through the land
to strike down the Egyptians, he will see
the blood and will pass over that doorway.
He will not let the destroyer enter
your houses and strike you down."
The Israelites did just what God said.

At midnight God struck down all the firstborn.
There was loud wailing in Egypt, for there
was not a house without someone dead.
Pharaoh called Moses and said,
"Up! Leave my people.
Take your flocks and herds, and go."

The Israelites Leave Egypt

Exodus 12–13

So the Israelites left Egypt.
There were about 600,000 men,
besides women and children.
The Egyptians urged the people to hurry.
"Otherwise," they said, "we will all die!"
By day God went ahead of the Israelites in a pillar
of cloud and by night in a pillar of fire.
So the Israelites could travel by day or night.

Crossing the Red Sea

Exodus 14

When Pharaoh was told that the Israelites had fled, he changed his mind and said, "What have I done?" So the Egyptians—all Pharaoh's horses and chariots, horsemen and troops— chased the Israelites.

As Pharaoh approached, the Israelites looked up, and there were the Egyptians!
They were terribly afraid.
They said to Moses, "What have you done?
It would have been better for us to serve the Egyptians than to die in the desert!"
Moses answered the people, "Don't be afraid.
God will fight for you."

Then Moses stretched out
his hand over the sea.
All that night God drove the sea back.
It turned into dry land.

The Israelites went through the sea
on dry ground, with a wall of water
on their right and on their left.

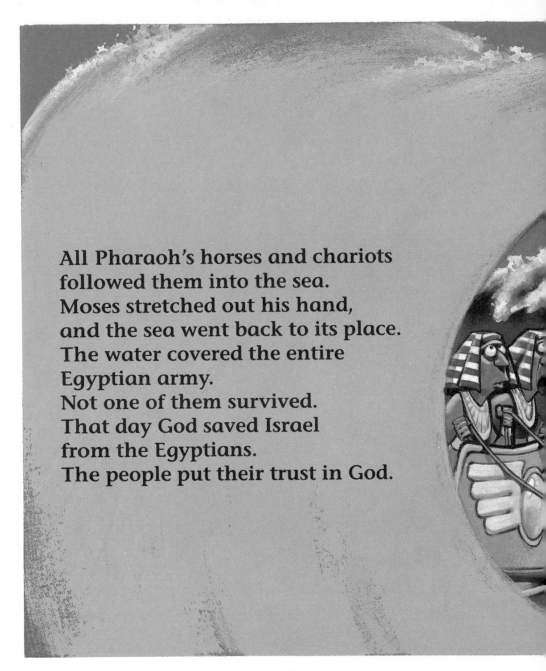

All Pharaoh's horses and chariots
followed them into the sea.
Moses stretched out his hand,
and the sea went back to its place.
The water covered the entire
Egyptian army.
Not one of them survived.
That day God saved Israel
from the Egyptians.
The people put their trust in God.

Manna and Quail
Exodus 16

The Israelites grumbled to Moses.
"In Egypt we ate all the food we wanted.
But you have brought us
to this desert to starve to death."

God said to Moses, "I have heard
the grumbling of the Israelites.
Tell them, 'Tonight you will eat meat,
and in the morning, bread.'"
That evening quail came and covered the camp.

In the morning thin flakes like frost appeared on the ground.
Moses said to the people, "It is the bread God has given you to eat."
The Israelites ate manna for forty years, until they came to the land of Canaan.

Moses at Mount Sinai

Exodus 19–20; 24

Three months after the Israelites left Egypt
they came to the Desert of Sinai. They camped
in the desert in front of the mountain.

A thick cloud hung over the mountain.
There was thunder and lightning,
and a very loud trumpet blast sounded.
Everyone in the camp trembled.

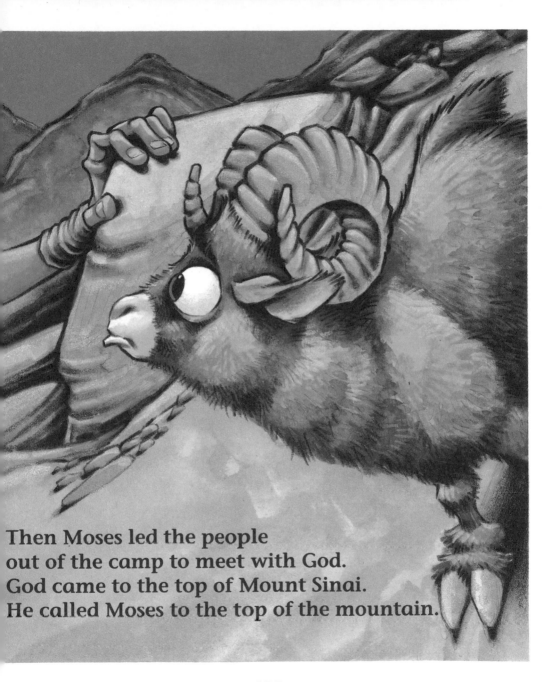

Then Moses led the people
out of the camp to meet with God.
God came to the top of Mount Sinai.
He called Moses to the top of the mountain.

And God spoke all these words:

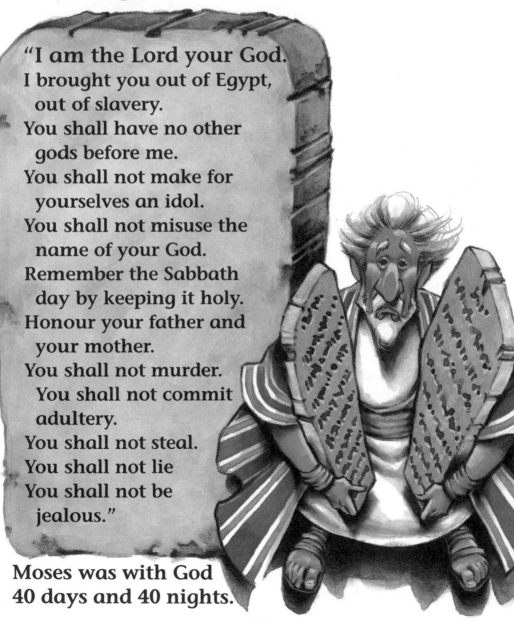

"I am the Lord your God.
I brought you out of Egypt,
   out of slavery.
You shall have no other
   gods before me.
You shall not make for
   yourselves an idol.
You shall not misuse the
   name of your God.
Remember the Sabbath
   day by keeping it holy.
Honour your father and
   your mother.
You shall not murder.
   You shall not commit
   adultery.
You shall not steal.
You shall not lie
You shall not be
   jealous."

Moses was with God
40 days and 40 nights.

The Golden Calf

Exodus 32–34

When the people saw that Moses was so long
in coming down from the mountain,
they went to Aaron and said,
"Make us gods who will lead us.
We don't know what has happened to Moses."

Aaron answered, "Take off your gold earrings.
Bring them to me."
Aaron made the gold into an idol
in the shape of a calf.
Then the people said,
"These are your gods, O Israel!"
And they ate and drank
and danced around the idol.

Then God said to Moses, "Go! Your people have made an idol in the shape of a calf."

138

Moses went down the mountain
with two tablets in his hands.
The tablets were the work of God.
When Moses approached the camp and saw
the calf and the dancing, he was very angry.

He threw down the tablets, breaking them
to pieces. He took the calf they had made
and burned it in the fire.
Then Moses said to the people,
"You have done a great sin. But I will go to God;
I will ask for his forgiveness."

Water From the Rock

Exodus 17

The Israelites camped,
but there was no water to drink.
The people quarrelled with Moses.
They said, "Give us water to drink.
Why did you bring us out of Egypt
to make us die of thirst?"
Then Moses cried out to God,
"What am I to do with these people?
They are almost ready to stone me."

God answered Moses,
"Walk ahead of the people.
I will stand before you by the rock
at Horeb. Strike the rock.
Water will come out of it
for the people to drink."
So Moses did this in the sight of Israel.

The Bronze Snake

Numbers 21

The Israelites spoke against God and said,
"Why have you brought us out of Egypt
to die in the desert? There is no bread!
There is no water! We hate this miserable food!"
Then God sent poisonous snakes.
They bit the people and many died.
The people came to Moses and said,
"We sinned. Ask God to take the snakes away."
So Moses prayed for the people.
God said to Moses, "Make a snake.
Put it up on a pole. Anyone who is bitten
can look at it and live."
So Moses put a bronze snake up on a pole.
When anyone was bitten by a snake and
looked at the bronze snake, he lived.

Exploring Canaan

Numbers 13–14

Moses sent twelve men to explore Canaan.
Moses said, "See what the land is like.
Are the people strong or weak?
What kind of towns do they live in?
How is the soil? Are there trees on it?"

The twelve men went and explored the land.
They cut a cluster of grapes.
Two of them carried it on a pole between them.
At the end of forty days they returned.

Ten of the men said,
"The land does flow with milk and honey!
But the people are powerful,
and the cities are very large.
We can't attack those people.
They are stronger than we are."

But two of the men, Joshua and Caleb, said,
"The land is good. God is with us.
Don't be afraid."

That night all the people grumbled,
"If only we had died in Egypt! Why is God
bringing us to this land only to let us be killed?"
Then God said, "Not one of you will
enter this land except Joshua and Caleb.
I will bring your children in to enjoy
the land you have rejected. For forty
years you will suffer in the desert."

The Fall of Jericho

Joshua 5–6

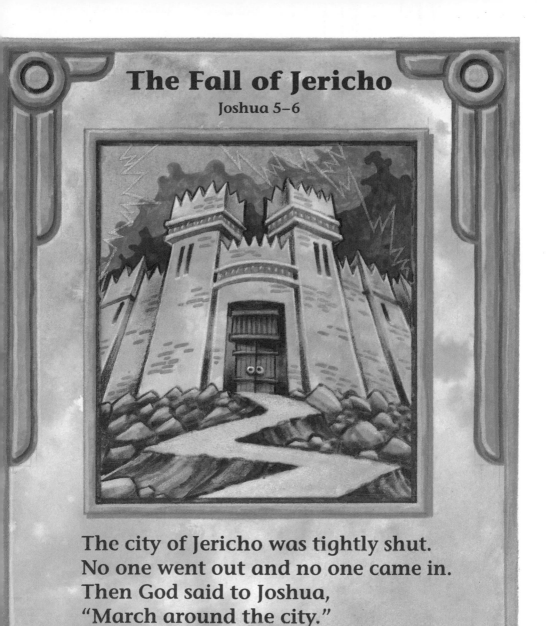

The city of Jericho was tightly shut.
No one went out and no one came in.
Then God said to Joshua,
"March around the city."

So Joshua ordered the people,
"Advance! March around the city."
So they marched around the city once and returne·
to the camp. They did this for six days.

On the seventh day, they got up at daybreak
and marched around the city seven times.
The seventh time around, Joshua commanded
the people, "Shout! For God has given you the city!"
When the trumpets sounded, the people shouted,
and the wall of the city fell down.
Every man ran straight in, and they took the city.

Gideon Fights the Midianites

Judges 7

Gideon and all his men camped near a spring.
The camp of the Midianites was north of them.
God said to Gideon, "You have too many men.
Anyone who is afraid may leave."
So 22,000 men left; 10,000 remained.

But God said to Gideon,
"There are still too many men."
So Gideon took the men down to the water.
Three hundred men drank
with their hands to their mouths.
All the rest got down on their knees to drink.
God said to Gideon, "With these 300 men
I will give the Midianites into your hands.
Let all the other men go home."

Gideon gave the 300 men trumpets
and empty jars with torches inside.
"Watch me," he told them. "Do exactly as I do.
They reached the edge of the camp
in the middle of the night.
They blew their trumpets and broke the jars.
They shouted, "A sword for the Lord and Gideo
All the Midianites ran, crying out as they fled.

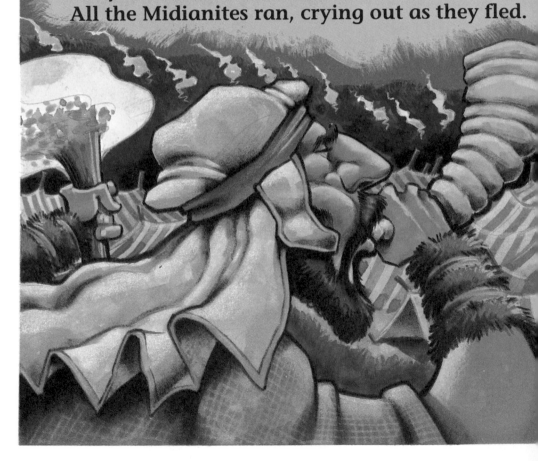

Samson and Delilah

Judges 13; 16

Samson was chosen by God to deliver
Israel from their enemy the Philistines.
Samson fell in love with Delilah.
The Philistines said to her,
"See if you can make him show you
the secret of his great strength."
So Delilah said to Samson, "Tell me
the secret of your great strength."

Samson said, "If you tie me with new ropes,
I'll become as weak as any other man."
So Delilah tied him up. Then she called,
"Samson, the Philistines are here!"
But Samson snapped the ropes.

Delilah then said to Samson, "You have been lying to me. Tell me how you can be tied." He replied, "If you weave my seven plaits into a loom, I'll become weak."
So while he was sleeping, Delilah wove his seven plaits into a loom.
Again she called to him,
"Samson, the Philistines are here!"
But he woke up and escaped the loom.

Then she nagged him
day after day until
he was tired to death.
So he told her everything.
"If my head were shaved,
I would become weak."

Having put Samson to sleep on her lap,
she called a man to shave off his hair.
And his strength left him.

Then the Philistines seized him,
gouged out his eyes and took him to prison.
But the hair on his head began to grow again.

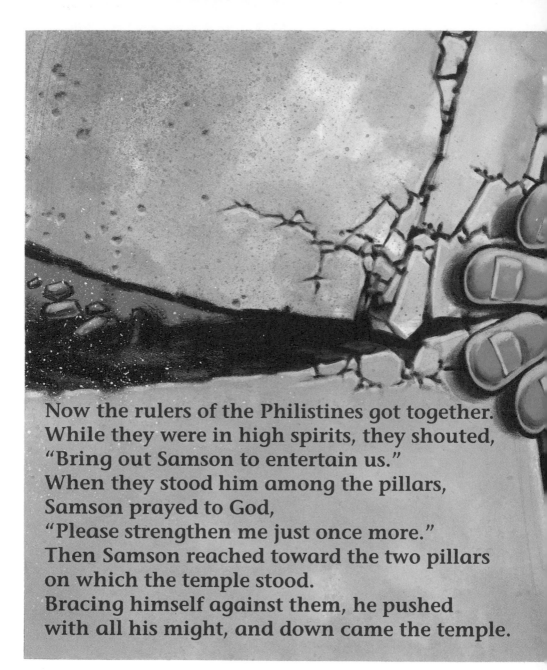

Now the rulers of the Philistines got together.
While they were in high spirits, they shouted,
"Bring out Samson to entertain us."
When they stood him among the pillars,
Samson prayed to God,
"Please strengthen me just once more."
Then Samson reached toward the two pillars
on which the temple stood.
Bracing himself against them, he pushed
with all his might, and down came the temple.

Naomi and Ruth

Ruth 1–4

There was a famine in the land.
A man, with his wife and two sons,
went to live for a while in Moab.

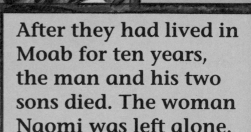

After they had lived in
Moab for ten years,
the man and his two
sons died. The woman
Naomi was left alone.

Naomi heard that there was food in Judah.

On the road to Judah, Naomi said to her sons' wives, "Go back to your mother's home. Find another husband."

Then one of the girls kissed Naomi good-by.

But Ruth clung to Naomi and said,
"I don't want to leave you.
Where you go I will go.
Where you stay I will stay.
Your people will be my people.
And your God my God."
So Naomi returned from Moab with Ruth.

JUDAH

MOAB

MT. NEBO

EDOM

BETHLEHEM

God Calls Samuel

1 Samuel 3

One night the priest Eli,
who could barely see, was lying down.
The boy Samuel was lying down also.
Then God called Samuel. And he ran to
Eli and said, "Here I am. You called me."
But Eli said, "I did not call. Go back and
lie down." So he went and lay down.

Again God called, "Samuel!"
And Samuel got up and went to Eli and said,
"Here I am. You called me."
"My son," Eli said, "I did not call.
Go back and lie down."
God called Samuel a third time,
and Samuel got up and went to Eli and said,
"Here I am. You called me."
Then Eli realized that God was calling.
So Eli told Samuel, "Go and lie down, and if
he calls you, say, 'Speak, for your servant is
listening.'" So Samuel went and lay down.

God came and called like the other times,
"Samuel! Samuel!"
Then Samuel said, "Speak,
for your servant is listening."
And God was with Samuel as he grew up.

Saul Made King

1 Samuel 10

Samuel brought all the tribes
of Israel together to choose a king.
Finally Saul was chosen.
But when the people looked for him,
they couldn't find him.
So they asked God,
"Is the man here?"
And God said,
"Yes, he's hiding
among the
baggage."

So the people ran and brought Saul out.
He was a head taller than any of the others.
Samuel said to all the people,
"Do you see the man God has chosen?
There is no one like him among all the people."
Then the people shouted, "Long live the king!"

Samuel Anoints David

1 Samuel 16

God said to Samuel, "Fill your horn with oil.
I am sending you to Jesse of Bethlehem.
I have chosen one of his sons to be king.
Anoint the one I show you."

When Samuel saw Jesse's son Eliab, he thought, "Surely he's the one I must anoint." But God said to Samuel, "Do not consider his appearance or his height, for I have rejected him. Man looks at the outward appearance, but God looks at the heart."

Jesse had seven of his sons pass before Samuel, but Samuel said to him, "God has not chosen these. Are these all the sons you have?" "There is still the youngest," Jesse answered, "but he is taking care of the sheep." Samuel said, "Send for him."

So Jesse sent for David.
He had a fine appearance and handsome features.
Then God said, "Anoint him. He's the one."
So Samuel took the horn of oil and anointed David.

David and Goliath

1 Samuel 17

The Philistines and the Israelites
got ready for war.
The Philistines were on one hill
and the Israelites were on another.

A champion named Goliath came out of the Philistine camp. He was over nine feet tall. Goliath shouted to the Israelites, "Give me a man and let us fight each other." All the Israelites were terrified. For forty days Goliath came forward every morning and every evening.

179

Now David's three oldest brothers
had followed King Saul to the war.
David was the youngest.
He took care of his father's sheep.
One day his father said to him,
"Take these ten loaves of bread to your brothers.
See how they are."

When David reached the camp he ran to the battle lines and greeted his brothers. As he was talking with them, Goliath shouted his usual threat.

And David heard it.

David said to Saul, "I'll fight him."
Saul replied, "You're only a boy."
But David said to Saul, "I've killed
the lion and the bear. God will deliver me
from the hand of this Philistine."

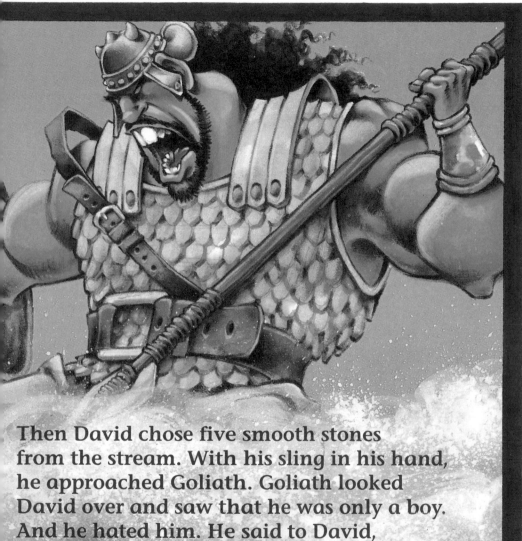

Then David chose five smooth stones
from the stream. With his sling in his hand,
he approached Goliath. Goliath looked
David over and saw that he was only a boy.
And he hated him. He said to David,
"Am I a dog, that you come at me with sticks?"

David said, "You come against me with sword
and spear. But I come against you
in the name of the Lord Almighty."
David ran to meet Goliath.
Taking out a stone, he slung it and struck Goliath.
The stone sank into his forehead,
and he fell facedown on the ground.
When the Philistines saw that their hero was dead,
they ran away.

Solomon Asks for Wisdom

1 Kings 3

When the time came for David to die,
he made his son Solomon king.
God came to Solomon in a dream and said,
"Ask for whatever you want me to give you."
Solomon answered, "You have made me king.
But I do not know how to rule.
So give me a wise heart."
God was pleased with Solomon, so he said,
"I will do what you have asked.
Also, I will give you what you have not asked for—
both riches and honour."

187

A Wise Ruling
1 Kings 3

Two women came to Solomon.
One of them said, "My lord, this woman and I
live in the same house. We both had babies.
During the night this woman's son died.
So she got up in the middle of the night
and took my son while I was asleep.
The next morning, I got up to nurse my son—
and he was dead! But when I looked at him,
I saw that it wasn't my son."

The other woman said, "No! The living one
is my son. The dead one is yours."
And so they argued before the king.

Then Solomon said,
"Bring me a sword.
Cut the living child
in two. Give half
to one mother
and half to the other."
The woman whose
son was alive said,
"Please, my lord, give
her the living baby!
Don't kill him!"
But the other woman
said, "Neither I nor you
shall have him.
Cut him in two!"
Then the king
gave his ruling:
"Give the baby to
the first woman.
Don't kill him.
She is his mother."
When Israel heard the
decision Solomon
had given, they saw
that he had wisdom
from God.

Solomon Builds the Temple

1 Kings 6

Solomon built a beautiful temple for God.
In building the temple,
only stone cut at the quarry was used.
No hammer, chisel or iron tool was heard
at the temple site while it was being built.
The inside of the temple was cedar,
carved with gourds and open flowers.
Solomon covered the inside
of the temple with pure gold.
He also covered the altar with gold.
On the walls all around the temple, he
carved angels, palm trees and flowers.
Finally the temple was finished.
Solomon had spent seven years building it.

Elijah Fed by Ravens

1 Kings 17

Many bad kings ruled Israel after Solomon.
They did not love God or follow him.
They worshipped idols. So God sent
his prophet, Elijah, to warn King Ahab,
"There will be neither dew
nor rain in the next few years."
Then God told Elijah: "Hide in the ravine.
You will drink from the brook,
and the ravens will feed you there."
Elijah did what God told him.
He went to the ravine and stayed there.
The ravens brought him bread and meat
in the morning and in the evening.
And he drank from the brook.

195

The Widow at Zarephath

1 Kings 17

The brook Elijah lived at dried up because there ha
been no rain. Then God told Elijah: "Go to Zarepha
I have commanded a widow there to feed you."

So Elijah went to Zarephath.
When he came to the town gate,
a widow was there gathering sticks.

Elijah called to her, "Would you bring me
water to drink? And a piece of bread?"
"I don't have any bread," she replied,
"only a handful of flour and a little oil.
I am gathering a few sticks to take home
and make a meal for myself and my son.
We will eat it—and then we'll die."
Elijah said, "Don't be afraid. Go home
and do as you have said. But first make
bread from what you have and bring it to me.
Then make something for yourself and your son.
The jar of flour will not be used up
and the jug of oil will not run dry
until the day God gives rain on the land."

She went away and did as Elijah told her.
So there was food every day for Elijah
and for the woman and her family.

Elijah on Mount Carmel

1 Kings 18

King Ahab went to meet Elijah. Elijah said to him, "You have forgotten God and followed Baal. Call the people from all over Israel to meet me on Mount Carmel. And bring the 450 prophets of Baal."

So they all gathered on Mount Carmel.
Elijah said to the people,
"If the Lord is God, follow him;
but if Baal is God, follow him."
The people said nothing.

Then Elijah said, "Get two bulls.
Put each bull on wood but don't set it on fire.
You call to your god. I'll call to the Lord.
The god who answers by fire—he is God."

So the 450 prophets of Baal called
to Baal from morning till noon.
"O Baal, answer us!" they shouted.
But no one answered.

At noon Elijah began to mock them.
"Shout louder!" he said. "Perhaps he is sleeping."

So they shouted louder and cut themselves.
Afternoon passed.
They continued their frantic praying.
But no one answered, no one paid attention.

Now it was Elijah's turn.
He dug a large trench around the altar.
Then he said to the people,
"Fill four large jars with water
and pour it on the offering and on the wood."
They did it three times, until the water
ran down the altar and filled the trench.

Then Elijah prayed: "Answer me, O God,
so these people will know that you are God."
Then fire fell from heaven and burned up
the bull, the wood, the stones, the soil,
and all the water in the trench.
When the people saw this, they cried,
"The Lord—he is God!"

Elijah Taken Up to Heaven

1 Kings 19; 2 Kings 2

Elisha followed Elijah and became his helper.
As they were walking along and talking together,
suddenly a chariot of fire and horses of fire
appeared and separated them.
And Elijah went up to heaven in a whirlwind.
Elisha saw this and yelled, "My father! My father!
The chariots and horsemen of Israel!"
And Elisha saw Elijah no more.

Naaman Healed of Leprosy

2 Kings 5

Naaman was commander
of the army of Aram.
He was a brave soldier,
but he had leprosy.

A young girl from Israel
was a servant to Naaman's wife.
She said to her mistress, "If only my
master would see the prophet Elisha!
He would cure him of his leprosy."

Naaman went to the king and told him what the
girl had said. "By all means, go," the king replied.

So Naaman went to Elisha's house.
Elisha sent a messenger to say to him,
"Go, wash yourself seven times in the Jordan.
Your skin will be like new. You will be cured."

But Naaman went away angry and said,
"I thought that he would call to his God,
wave his hand and cure me of my leprosy."
So he went off in a rage.

Naaman's servants said, "If the prophet had told you to do some great thing, wouldn't you have done it? How much more, then, when he tells you to wash and be clean?"

So Naaman dipped himself in the Jordan seven times. And his skin became clean like that of a young boy.

Then Naaman went back to Elisha and said,
"Now I know that there is no God
in all the world except in Israel."

Joash Repairs the Temple

2 Chronicles 24

Joash was seven years old when he became king.
He reigned in Jerusalem forty years.
Joash did what was right in the eyes of God.
Wicked men had broken into the temple.
So Joash decided to restore it.
A chest was placed outside the temple.
All the people brought their money gladly.
They collected a great amount of money.

The king gave it to the men who carried out the
work. They hired workers to repair the temple.
The men in charge worked hard.
They rebuilt the temple, and it was beautiful again.

The Shepherd's Psalm

Psalm 23

The Lord is my shepherd, I shall not be in want.
He makes me lie down in green pastures,
he leads me beside quiet waters,
he restores my soul.
He guides me in paths of righteousness
for his name's sake.
Even though I walk
through the valley of the shadow of death,
I will fear no evil,
for you are with me;
your rod and your staff,
they comfort me.

You prepare a table before me
in the presence of my enemies.
You anoint my head with oil;
my cup overflows.
Surely goodness and love will follow me
all the days of my life,
and I will dwell in the house of the Lord
forever.

A Worship Psalm

Psalm 100

Shout for joy to the Lord all the earth.
  Worship the Lord with gladness;
    come before him with joyful songs.
Know that the Lord is God.
  It is he who made us, and we are his;
    we are his people, the sheep of his pasture.
Enter his gates with thanksgiving
  and his courts with praise;
    give thanks to him and praise his name.
For the Lord is good and his love endures forever;
  his faithfulness continues through
    all generations.

A Praise Psalm

Psalm 150

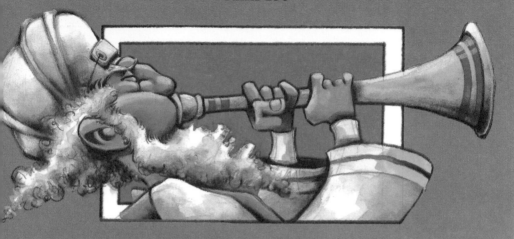

Praise the Lord.
Praise God in his sanctuary;
  praise him in his mighty heavens.
Praise him for his acts of power;
  praise him for his surpassing greatness.
Praise him with the sounding of the trumpet,
  praise him with the harp and lyre,
praise him with tambourine and dancing,
  praise him with the strings and flute,
praise him with the clash of cymbals,
  praise him with resounding cymbals.
Let everything that has breath praise the Lord.
Praise the Lord.

A Time for Everything

Ecclesiastes 3

There is a time for everything,
   and a season for every activity under heaven:
   a time to be born and a time to die,
   a time to plant and a time to uproot,
   a time to kill and a time to heal,
   a time to tear down and a time to build,
   a time to weep and a time to laugh,
   a time to mourn and a time to dance,
   a time to scatter stones and a time to gather them,
   a time to embrace and a time to refrain,
   a time to search and a time to give up,
   a time to keep and
      a time to throw away,
   a time to tear and
      a time to mend,
   a time to be silent and
      a time to speak,
   a time to love and
      a time to hate,
   a time for war and
      a time for peace.

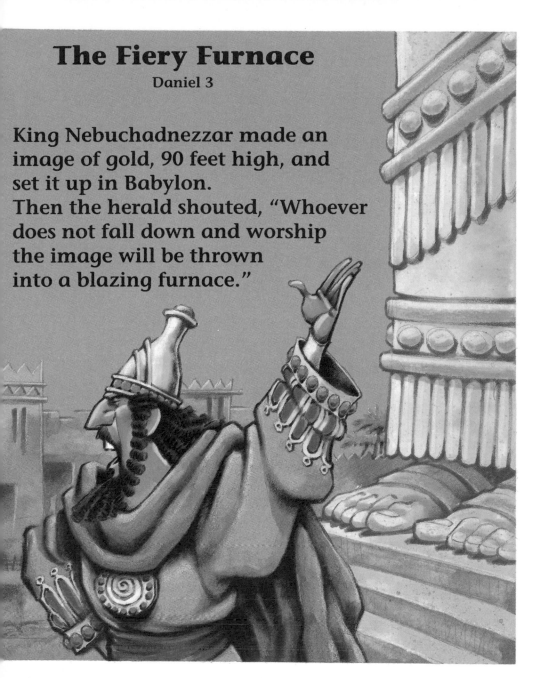

The Fiery Furnace

Daniel 3

King Nebuchadnezzar made an
image of gold, 90 feet high, and
set it up in Babylon.
Then the herald shouted, "Whoever
does not fall down and worship
the image will be thrown
into a blazing furnace."

Some men said to Nebuchadnezzar,
"Some Jews—Shadrach, Meshach and Abednego—
do not worship the image of gold."

Furious with rage, Nebuchadnezzar said to
Shadrach, Meshach and Abednego,
"If you do not worship the image,
you will be thrown into a blazing furnace.,
Then what god will rescue you?"
The three men replied, "If we are thrown
into the furnace, God is able to save us.
But even if he does not we will not
worship the image of gold."

Then Nebuchadnezzar ordered the furnace
heated seven times hotter than usual.
He commanded some of his strongest soldiers
to throw the men into the blazing furnace.
The furnace was so hot that
the flames killed the soldiers.

Shadrach, Meshach and Abednego,
firmly tied, fell into the blazing furnace.
Then Nebuchadnezzar leaped to his feet.
"Look! I see four men walking around in the fire.
And the fourth looks like an angel."

Then Nebuchadnezzar shouted,
"Shadrach, Meshach and Abednego, come here!"
So the men came out of the fire.
The fire had not harmed their bodies.
The fire had not burned a hair of their heads.
Their robes were not burned,
and there was no smell of fire on them.

Then Nebuchadnezzar said,
"Praise be to the God of Shadrach, Meshach and
Abednego! No other god can save in this way."

The Writing on the Wall

Daniel 5

King Belshazzar gave a great banquet.
He gave orders to bring in the gold
and silver goblets that Nebuchadnezzar
had taken from the temple in Jerusalem.
As the king and his guests drank wine from them,
they praised the gods of gold and silver.

Suddenly the fingers of a human hand
appeared and wrote on the wall.
The king watched the hand as it wrote.
His face turned pale.
He was so frightened that his knees
knocked together and his legs gave way.
All the king's wise men could not tell
the king what the writing meant.

233

So Daniel was brought before the king.
Then Daniel said, "This is what these words mean
God has numbered the days of your reign
and brought it to an end.
Your kingdom is divided and given
to the Medes and Persians."

Then Daniel was clothed in purple,
and a gold chain was placed around his neck.
He was made a ruler in the kingdom.
That same night Belshazzar was killed,
and Darius the Mede took over the kingdom.

Daniel in the Den of Lions

Daniel 6

Daniel went home to his upstairs room where the windows opened toward Jerusalem. Three times a day he got down on his knees and prayed, giving thanks to God.

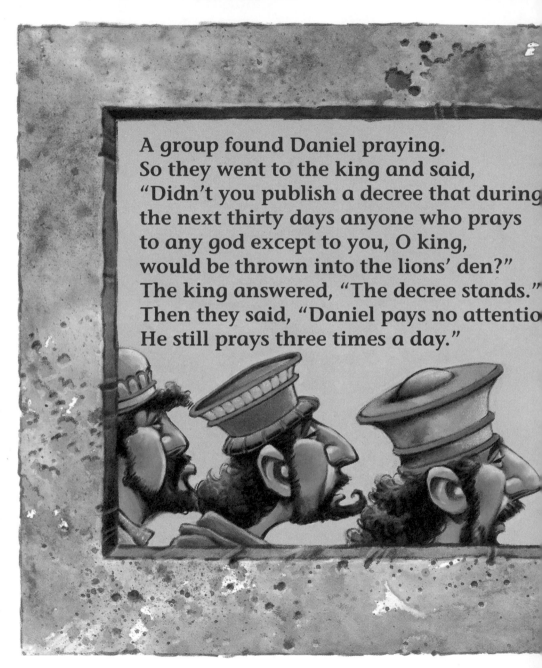

A group found Daniel praying.
So they went to the king and said,
"Didn't you publish a decree that during
the next thirty days anyone who prays
to any god except to you, O king,
would be thrown into the lions' den?"
The king answered, "The decree stands."
Then they said, "Daniel pays no attentio
He still prays three times a day."

So the king gave the order. They brought
Daniel and threw him into the lions' den.
The king said to Daniel,
"May your God rescue you!"

Then the king returned to his palace
and spent the night without eating.
And he could not sleep.
At dawn, the king got up
and hurried to the lions' den.

When he came near the den, he called to Daniel, "Daniel, has your God been able to rescue you from the lions?"

Daniel answered, "My God sent his angel, and he shut the mouths of the lions. They have not hurt me."
The king was overjoyed and gave orders to lift Daniel out of the den.

Jonah and the Great Fish

Jonah 1–2

God said to Jonah, "Go to the great city of Nineveh and preach." But Jonah ran away. He went aboard a ship and sailed for Tarshish.

245

Then God sent a great wind on the sea.
The ship was about to break up in the storm.
All the sailors were afraid.
Each cried out to his own god.

But Jonah had gone below deck,
where he fell into a deep sleep.
The captain went to him and said,
"How can you sleep?
Get up and call on your god!"

The sea was getting rougher and rougher.
So the sailors asked Jonah,
"What should we do to make the sea calm down?"
"Throw me into the sea," he replied,
"and it will become calm. It's my fault
that this great storm has come upon you."
Instead, the men did their best to row back to land.
But they could not, for the sea grew even wilder.

Then they took Jonah and threw him overboard.
The raging sea grew calm.
At this the men greatly feared God.
And God sent a great fish to swallow Jonah.

Jonah was inside the fish
three days and three nights.
From inside the fish he prayed to God.
And God commanded the fish
to vomit Jonah onto dry land.

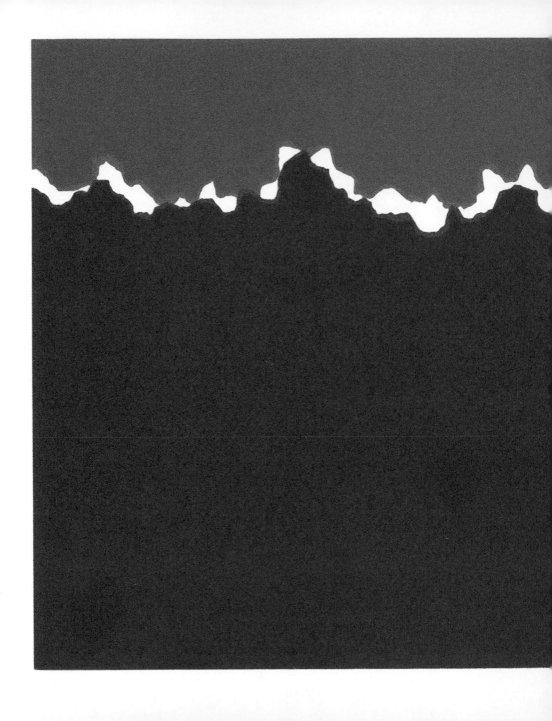

NEW
TESTAMENT

Mary and the Angel

Luke 1

God sent an angel to Mary, who was a virgin.
She was preparing to marry a man named Joseph.
The angel went to Mary and said,
"Greetings. God is with you."
Mary was very troubled.
But the angel said, "Don't be afraid, Mary,
you have found favour with God.
You will give birth to a son.
You are to give him the name Jesus."

"How will this be?" Mary asked.
The angel answered, "The Holy Spirit
will come upon you. The holy one to be born
will be called the Son of God.
Nothing is impossible with God."

"I am God's servant," Mary answered.
"May all this happen to me just as you have said."
Then the angel left.

Jesus Is Born

Luke 2

Caesar Augustus announced that a census should be taken of the entire Roman world. Everyone went to his own town to register.

Joseph and Mary went to Bethlehem, the town of David. Mary was to be married Joseph and was expecting a child.

While Mary and Joseph were in Bethlehem,
the time came for the baby to be born.
And she gave birth to her firstborn, a son.
She wrapped him in cloths
and placed him in a manger,
because there was no room for them in the inn.

259

The Shepherds and the Angels
Luke 2

Outside of Bethlehem, shepherds were living in the fields, watching their sheep at night.

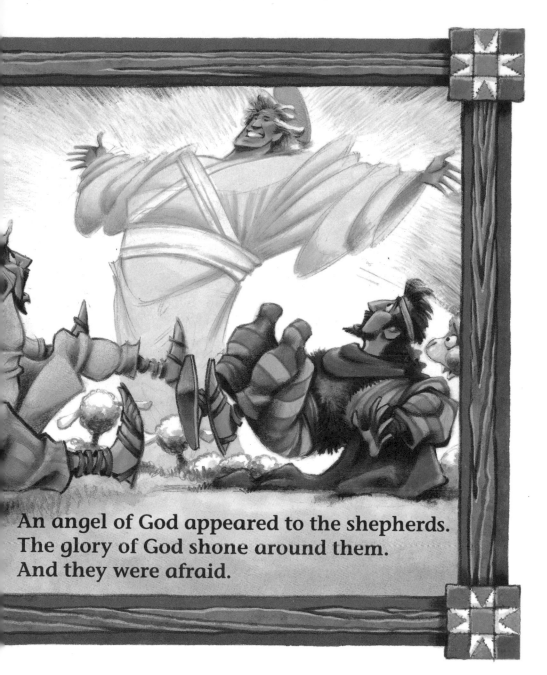

An angel of God appeared to the shepherds.
The glory of God shone around them.
And they were afraid.

But the angel said to them, "Don't be afraid.
I bring you good news of great joy
that will be for all the people.
Today in Bethlehem a Saviour has been born.
He is Christ the Lord. You will find a baby
wrapped in cloths and lying in a manger."

Suddenly many, many angels appeared,
praising God and saying,
"Glory to God in the highest, and on earth peace."

When the angels had left them,
the shepherds hurried to Bethlehem.

They found Mary and Joseph and the baby,
who was lying in the manger.

When they had seen the baby Jesus,
they told everyone about him.
And everyone who heard the story
was amazed at what the shepherds said.

Jesus Is Presented in the Temple

Luke 2

Joseph and Mary took Jesus to Jerusalem
to present him to God.
Now there was a man in Jerusalem called Simeon.
The Holy Spirit had told him that he would
see the Christ before he died.
Moved by the Spirit, Simeon went to the temple.
When Mary and Joseph brought in Jesus,
Simeon took him in his arms and praised God.

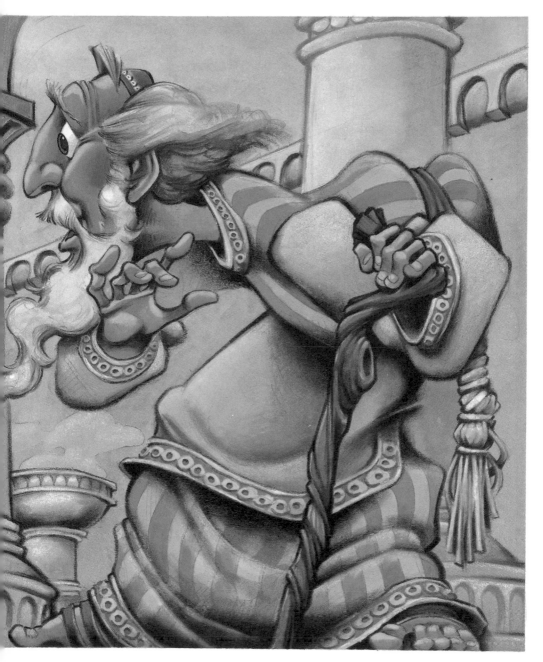

There was also an old woman, Anna.
She never left the temple but
worshipped and prayed night and day.
Coming up to Mary and Joseph,
she gave thanks to God for the child.

Joseph and Mary returned to their own town of Nazareth. There Jesus grew and became strong. He was filled with wisdom, and the grace of God was upon him.

The Magi Visit Jesus

Matthew 2

After Jesus was born in Bethlehem,
Magi from the east came to Jerusalem.
"Where is the one who has been born
king of the Jews?" they asked.
"We saw his star in the east.
We have come to worship him."

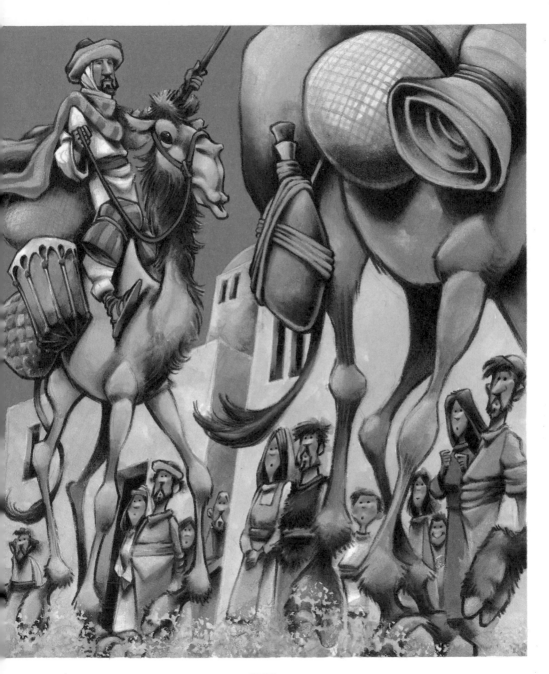

When King Herod heard this he was upset.

He called the Magi secretly and found out the exact time the star had appeared.

He sent them to Bethlehem and said, "Make a careful search for the child. As soon as you find him, report to me, so that I too may go and worship him."

The Magi went on their way.
The star went ahead of the Magi until it stopped
over the place where the child lived.
When they saw the star they were overjoyed.

Coming to the house, they saw
Jesus with his mother Mary.
They bowed down and worshipped him.
Then they presented him with gifts of gold
and of incense and of myrrh.

God told them in a dream not to go back to Herod.
And they returned to their country by another way.

The Escape to Egypt

Matthew 2

When the Magi had gone,
an angel appeared to Joseph in a dream.
"Get up," he said, "take the child and
his mother and escape to Egypt.
Stay there until I tell you, for Herod is
going to search for the child to kill him."

So Joseph got up, took Jesus and his mother during the night and left for Egypt.
They stayed there until the death of Herod.

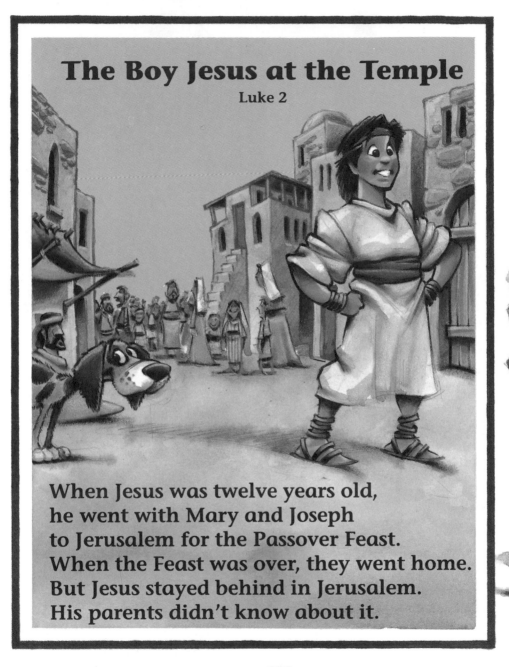

The Boy Jesus at the Temple

Luke 2

When Jesus was twelve years old,
he went with Mary and Joseph
to Jerusalem for the Passover Feast.
When the Feast was over, they went home.
But Jesus stayed behind in Jerusalem.
His parents didn't know about it.

They thought he was in their company,
so Mary and Joseph travelled for a day.
Then they began to look for him.
When they couldn't find him, they went back
to Jerusalem to look for him.

After three days Mary and Joseph
found Jesus in the temple.
He was sitting with the teachers,
listening to them and asking them questions.
Everyone who heard Jesus was amazed
at his understanding and his answers.

When Jesus' parents saw him, they were surprised.
His mother said, "Son, why have you
treated us like this? Your father and I
have been anxiously searching for you."
"Why were you searching for me?" he asked.
"Didn't you know I had to be
in my Father's house?"
But Mary and Joseph did not
understand what he was saying.

Then Jesus went home with Mary and Joseph
and obeyed them. He grew in wisdom and stature,
and in favour with God and men.

John the Baptist

Matthew 3; Mark 1

John the Baptist preached in the desert.
The people of Jerusalem were baptized
by him in the Jordan River.

John wore clothing made of camel's hair,
with a leather belt around his waist.
He ate locusts and wild honey.
This was his message:
"After me will come one more powerful than I.
I baptize you with water,
but he will baptize you with the Holy Spirit."

John Baptizes Jesus

Matthew 3; Luke 3

Then Jesus came to the Jordan River
to be baptized by John.

As soon as Jesus was baptized,
he came up out of the water.
At that moment, heaven opened and
the Holy Spirit came down on him like a dove.
A voice from heaven said, "You are my Son,
whom I love; I am well pleased with you."

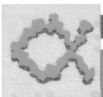

Jesus Calls the First Disciples

Matthew 4; Mark 2

As Jesus was walking beside the Sea of Galilee
he saw two brothers, Peter and Andrew.
They were fishermen, and
they were throwing a net into the lake.
"Come, follow me," Jesus said,
"and I will make you fishers of men."
At once they left their nets and followed him.

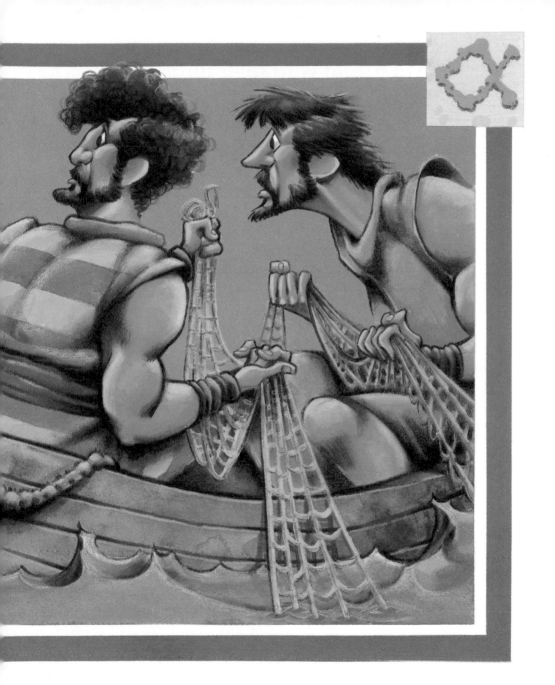

Later, Jesus saw two other brothers, James and John. They were in a boat with their father, preparing their nets. Jesus called them. Immediately they left the boat and their father and followed him.

Once again Jesus went out beside the lake. As he walked along, he saw Levi sitting at the tax collector's booth. "Follow me," Jesus told him. And Levi got up and followed him.

Jesus Changes Water to Wine

John 2

A wedding took place at a town called Cana. Mary, Jesus' mother, was there. Jesus and his disciples were also invited to the wedding.

When the wine was gone, Jesus' mother said to him,
"They have no more wine."
Then she said to the servants,
"Do whatever he tells you."
Nearby stood six large stone water jars.
Jesus said to the servants, "Fill the jars with water."
So they filled them to the brim.

Then he told them, "Now pour some out
and take it to the master of the banquet."
The master of the banquet tasted the water
that had been turned into wine.
Then he said to the bridegroom,
"You have saved the best wine till now."
This was Jesus' first miracle.

How to Pray

Matthew 5–6

Jesus went up on a mountainside and sat down.
His disciples came to him,
and he began to teach them.
"This is how you should pray," Jesus said.

"Our Father in heaven, hallowed be your name,
your kingdom come, your will be done
   on earth as it is in heaven.
Give us today our daily bread.
Forgive us our debts,
   as we also have forgiven our debtors.
And lead us not into temptation,
but deliver us from the evil one,
for yours is the kingdom and the power
      and the glory forever. Amen."

Jesus Heals a Lame Man

Mark 2; Luke 5

One day Jesus was teaching.
Some men came carrying a man who couldn't walk
But they could not get the man to Jesus
because the crowd was so big.

The men made an opening in the roof above Jesus.
They lowered the lame man on his mat
through the roof into the middle of the crowd,
   right in front of Jesus.

301

When Jesus saw their faith,
he said to the lame man,
"Get up, take your mat and go home."

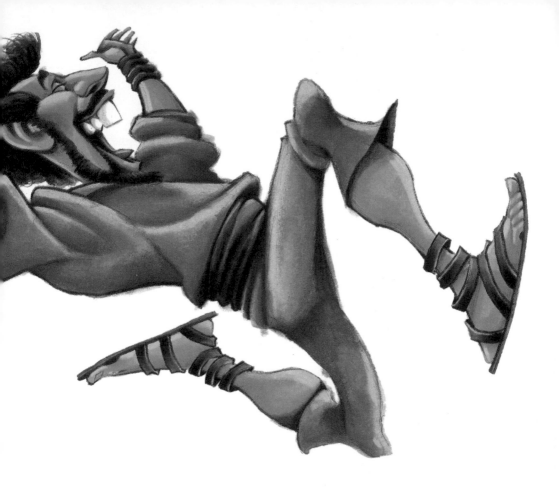

The man got up, took his mat
and went home praising God.
Everyone was amazed. They praised God, saying,
"We have never seen anything like this!"

Jesus Calms the Storm

Matthew 8; Mark 4; Luke 8

One day Jesus said to his disciples,
"Let's go over to the other side of the lake."

So they got into a boat and
set out. Without warning, a
furious storm came up.
The waves swept over the boat.
But Jesus was sleeping.

The disciples woke him and said,
"Lord, save us! We're going to drown!"

Jesus got up and said to the wind and the waves,
"Quiet! Be still!" Then the wind died down,
and it was completely calm.

Jesus said to his disciples,
"Why are you so afraid?
Do you still have no faith?"

They were terrified and asked each other,
"Who is this? Even the wind
and the waves obey him!"

A Dead Girl Comes Alive

Matthew 9; Mark 5; Luke 8

A ruler, named Jairus, knelt before Jesus and said, "My little daughter has just died. Please come and put your hands on her, and she will live."
So Jesus went with him.

When Jesus entered the ruler's house and saw the noisy crowd, he said, "Go away. The girl isn't dead but asleep." But they laughed at him.

He took the little girl's mother and father
and went in where the child was.
He took her by the hand and said,
"Little girl, get up!"

Immediately the girl stood up and walked around.
All those in the house were completely astonished.

Jesus Feeds 5,000

Matthew 14; Mark 6; Luke 9; John 6

When Jesus saw a big crowd,
he felt sorry for them.
He healed the ones who were sick.

Late in the day the disciples said to Jesus,
"Send the people away so
they can buy something to eat."
But Jesus said, "They don't need to go away.
You give them something to eat."

One of the disciples, Andrew, spoke up.

"Here's a boy with five loaves and two fish. But how can that feed this many people?"

314

There was plenty of grass in
that place, so the men sat down.
Jesus then gave thanks.
The disciples gave the bread
and the fish to the people.

When all the people had enough to eat,
Jesus said, "Pick up the pieces
that are left over. Don't waste any."

The disciples filled twelve baskets
with the leftover bread and fish.
The number of those who ate
was about 5,000 men,
besides women and children.

Jesus Walks on Water

Matthew 14; Mark 6; John 6

Jesus made his disciples get into their boat
and go on ahead of him to Bethsaida.
He then went into the hills to pray.

When evening came, the boat was in the middle
of the lake, and Jesus was alone on land.
He saw the disciples straining at the oars,
because the wind was against them.

Jesus went out to the disciples, walking on the water.
When they saw him, they thought he was a ghost.
And they were terrified!

Jesus immediately called to them: "Take courage! It is I. Don't be afraid."

"Lord, if it's you," Peter replied, "tell me to come out to you on the water."

"Come," Jesus said.

Then Peter got out of the boat and walked on the water to Jesus.

But when he saw the wind, he was afraid.

He began to sink and cried out, "Lord, save me!"

Immediately Jesus reached out his hand and caught him.

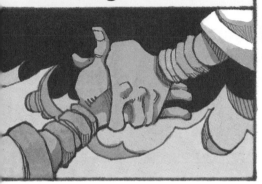

When they climbed into the boat, the wind died down.

Then the others in the boat worshipped Jesus, saying, "Truly you are the Son of God."

Jesus told this story to the people:

The Story of the Good Samaritan
Luke 10

A man was going from Jerusalem to Jericho, when he fell into the hands of robbers.

They stripped him of his clothes. They beat him and went away, leaving him half dead.

A priest happened to be going down the same road. When he saw the man, he passed by on the other side.

A Levite also passed by on the other side.

But when a Samaritan came and saw the man, he felt sorry for him, and he bandaged his wounds. The Samaritan put the man on his own donkey. He took him to an inn and took care of him.

The next day the Samaritan gave two silver coins to the innkeeper. "Look after him," he said. "When I return, I will pay you for any extra expense."

Jesus asked, "Which of these three was a neighbour to the man who fell into the hands of robbers?"
Those listening replied,
"The one who took care of him."
Jesus said, "Go and do likewise."

Jesus Visits Martha and Mary

Luke 10

Jesus and his disciples came to a village.
A woman named Martha opened her home to him.

Martha had a sister called Mary,
who sat at Jesus' feet listening to what he said.

But Martha was upset by all
the preparations that had to be made.

She came to Jesus and asked,
"Don't you care that my sister has
left me to do the work by myself?
Tell her to help me!"

"Martha, Martha," Jesus answered,
"you are worried and upset about many things.
But only one thing is needed.
Mary has chosen what is better,
and it will not be taken away from her."

Lazarus Is Raised to Life

John 11

A man named Lazarus was sick.
His sisters, Mary and Martha, sent word to Jesus,
"Lord, the one you love is sick."

Jesus loved Martha and Mary and Lazarus.
Yet when he heard that Lazarus was sick,
he stayed where he was two more days.
Then he said to his disciples,
"Let's go to Lazarus."

On his arrival, Jesus found that Lazarus
had already been in the tomb for four days.
Many people had come to
comfort Martha and Mary.
"Where have you laid him?" Jesus asked.
"Come and see, Lord," they replied.
Jesus wept, and the people said,
"See how he loved him!"

When Jesus came to the tomb, he said,
"Take away the stone."

"But, Lord," said Martha, "by this time
there's a bad smell. He's been there four days."

Then Jesus said, "Didn't I tell you that
if you believed, you would see the glory of God?"

So they took away the stone.

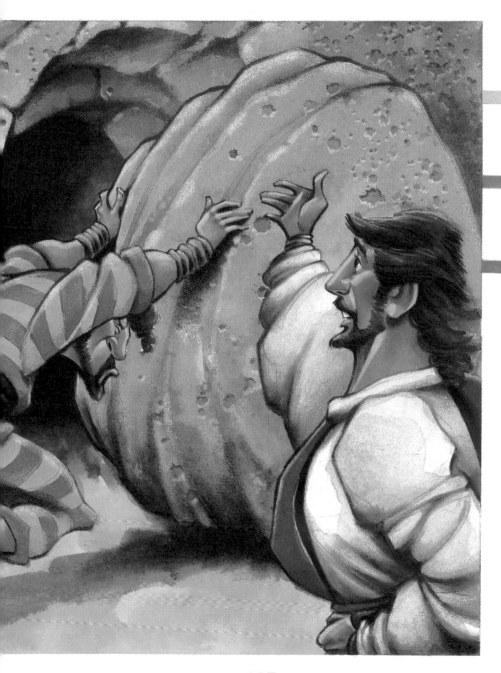

Jesus called in a loud voice, "Lazarus, come out!"
The dead man came out.
His hands and his feet were wrapped with
strips of linen and a cloth was around his face.
Jesus said to them, "Take off
the grave clothes and let him go."
Many of the people who had come to visit
Mary and Martha put their faith in Jesus.

The Story of the Lost Sheep

Luke 15

Jesus told the people this story:
Suppose a shepherd has 100 sheep
and loses one of them.
What does he do?
He leaves the 99 and goes after
the lost sheep until he finds it.
And when he finds it, he joyfully
puts it on his shoulders and goes home.

Then he calls his friends and neighbors together
and says, "Rejoice with me;
I have found my lost sheep."
In the same way there will be more rejoicing
in heaven over one sinner who repents
than over 99 righteous people
who do not need to repent.

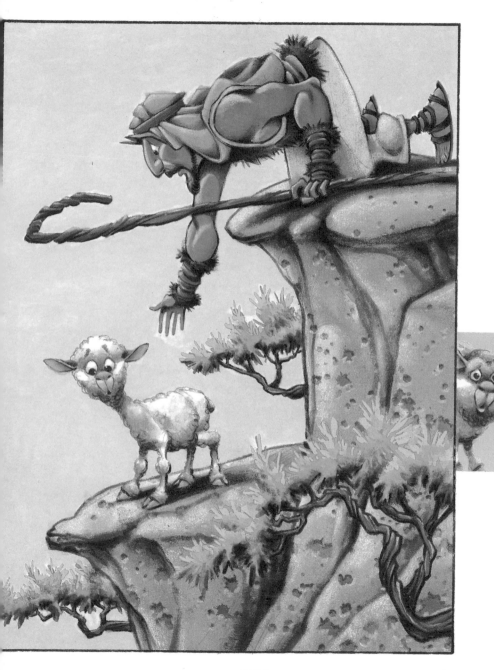

The Story of the Lost Coin

Luke 15

Jesus told the people this story:
Suppose a woman has ten silver coins and loses one
What does she do?
She lights a lamp, sweeps the house
and searches carefully until she finds it.

And when she finds it,
she calls her friends and
neighbours together and says,
"Rejoice with me; I have
found my lost coin."
In the same way there is
rejoicing in the presence
of the angels of God over
one sinner who repents.

The Story of the Lost Son

Luke 15

Jesus told the people this story:
A man had two sons.
The younger one said to his father,
"Father, give me my share of the estate."
And the father did.

Then the younger son got together
all he had and set off for a distant country.
There he wasted his wealth in wild living.

After he had spent everything, he was in need.
So he hired himself out to feed pigs.
He longed to fill his stomach with the pigs' food,
but no one gave him anything.

Then he thought to himself,
"How many of my father's hired men have
food to spare? And here I am starving to death!"
So he went to his father.

While the son was still a long way off, his father saw him.
He was filled with love for him.
He ran to his son, threw his arms around him and kissed him.

The son said, "Father, I have sinned. I am no longer worthy to be called your son."

But the father said to his servants, "Quick! Bring the best robe and put it on him. Put a ring on his finger and sandals on his feet. Bring the fattened calf and kill it. Let's have a feast and celebrate. My son was dead and is alive again. He was lost and is found."
So they began to celebrate.

Jesus Heals Ten Men

Luke 17

As Jesus was going into a village,
ten men who had leprosy met him.
They stood at a distance and called out,
"Jesus, Master, have pity on us!"

When Jesus saw them, he said,
"Go, show yourselves to the priests."
And as they went, they were healed.

When one of the men saw he was healed,
he came back, praising God.
He threw himself at Jesus' feet and thanked him.

Jesus asked, "Weren't ten healed?
Where are the other nine?"
Then Jesus said to the man, "Rise and go.
Your faith has made you well."

The Little Children and Jesus

Matthew 19; Mark 10; Luke 18

People were bringing
little children to Jesus
to have him touch them
and pray for them.
The disciples told the people to stop.
But Jesus called the children
to him and said,
"Let the little children come to me,
and do not stop them,
for the kingdom of God
belongs to such as these."
Jesus took the children in his arms.
He put his hands on them
and blessed them.

Zacchaeus

Luke 19

Zacchaeus was a very wealthy tax collector. He wanted to see Jesus, but because he was short, he couldn't see over the crowd.

So Zacchaeus ran ahead and
climbed a tree in order to see Jesus.
When Jesus reached the tree, he looked up and said,
"Zacchaeus, come down immediately.
I must stay at your house today."
So Zacchaeus came down and
welcomed Jesus at his home.

Jesus Enters Jerusalem

Matthew 21; Mark 11; Luke 19

As they approached Jerusalem, Jesus said to two
of his disciples, "Go to the village ahead of you.
As you enter it, you will find a colt tied there.
Untie it and bring it here.
If anyone asks you, 'Why are you doing this?'
tell him, 'Jesus needs it.'" The disciples went
and found a colt tied at a doorway.
As they untied it, some people asked,
"What are you doing?"
They answered as Jesus had told them to,
and the people let them go.

The disciples brought the colt to Jesus.
They threw their cloaks over the colt,
and Jesus sat on them. As Jesus entered the city,
many people spread their cloaks on the road.

Others cut branches from the trees
and spread them on the road.
The whole crowd began joyfully to praise God,
shouting, "Hosanna!"
"Blessed is he who comes in the name of the Lord!"
"Hosanna in the highest!"

Mary Honours Jesus

John 12

A dinner was given in Jesus' honour.
Martha served, while Lazarus was eating with Jesus.
Then Mary brought in some expensive perfume.

She poured the perfume on Jesus' feet
and wiped his feet with her hair.
The house was filled with
the beautiful smell of the perfume.

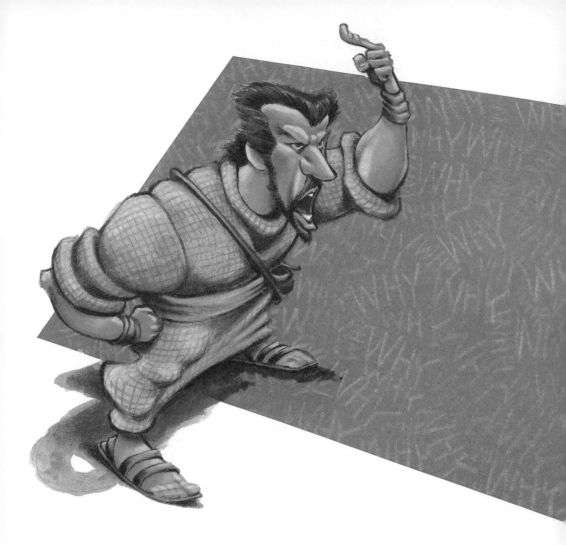

One of the disciples, Judas Iscariot, said,
"Why wasn't this perfume sold
and the money given to the poor?"
(Judas didn't say this because he cared
about the poor but because he was a thief.)

"Leave her alone," Jesus said.
"She did this to prepare me for my burial.
You'll always have the poor with you,
but you won't always have me."

Jesus Washes the Disciples' Feet

John 13

It was just before the Passover Feast.
The evening meal was being served.
Jesus got up from the meal
and wrapped a towel around his waist.

Then Jesus poured water into a basin and began to wash his disciples' feet. He dried their feet with the towel that was wrapped around him.

"Do you understand what I have done for you?"
he asked them. "Now that I,
your Lord and Teacher, have washed your feet,
you also should wash one another's feet.
Now that you know these things,
you will be blessed if you do them."

The Last Supper

Matthew 26; Mark 14

When the day came to celebrate the Passover Feast,
Jesus said to two of his disciples,
"Go into the city. A man carrying
a jar of water will meet you. Follow him.
He will show you a large upper room.
Make preparations for the Passover Feast there."

The disciples went into the city
and found things just as Jesus had told them.
So they prepared the Passover Feast.
When evening came,
Jesus arrived with the disciples.

While they were eating,
Jesus took bread,
gave thanks and broke it.
He gave it to his disciples, saying,
"Take and eat; this is my body."

372

Then he took the cup, gave thanks and offered it to them, and they all drank from it.

"This is my blood which is poured out for the forgiveness of sins," he said. When they had sung a hymn, they went out to Gethsemane.

Jesus Prays in Gethsemane

Matthew 26; Mark 14; Luke 22

Jesus went with his disciples to Gethsemane. He said to them, "Sit here while I pray."

He took Peter, James and John along with him,
and he knelt down and prayed, "Father,
if you are willing, take this cup from me.
Yet not my will, but yours be done."
An angel from heaven appeared
to him and strengthened him.

Then Jesus went back to the disciples
and found them sleeping.
"Why are you sleeping?" he asked.
"Get up and pray so that you will not
fall into temptation."
Jesus went away a second time
and prayed the same thing.
When he came back, he again
found the disciples sleeping.

So Jesus left them and prayed the third time, saying the same thing.
Then he returned to the disciples and said, "Are you still sleeping? Look, the hour is near, and I am about to be betrayed.
Rise, let's go! Here comes my betrayer!"

Jesus Is Arrested

Matthew 26; Mark 14; Luke 22; John 18

Now Judas, who betrayed Jesus,
knew the place called Gethsemane,
because Jesus often met there with his disciples.

Judas came, guiding a group of soldiers.
They were carrying torches, swords and clubs.

Jesus asked them, "Who is it you want?"
"Jesus of Nazareth," they replied.
"I am he," Jesus said.

Going to Jesus, Judas said, "Rabbi!"
and he kissed him.
Then Simon Peter drew his sword and
cut off the right ear of someone in the crowd.
Jesus said, "Put your sword away!"
And he touched the man's ear and healed him.

Then the soldiers seized Jesus and arrested him.
All the disciples deserted Jesus and ran away.

Pilate Tries Jesus

Matthew 27; Mark 15

Early in the morning, the priests and the elders decided to put Jesus to death.
They bound Jesus and handed him over to Pilate.

"Are you the king of the Jews?" asked Pilate.
"Yes," Jesus replied.

Now it was Pilate's custom at the Passover Feast
to release a prisoner chosen by the crowd.
So when the crowd had gathered, Pilate asked them
"Which one do you want me to release:
Barabbas, or Jesus?"
"Barabbas," they answered.

"What shall I do with Jesus?" Pilate asked.
"Crucify him!" they shouted.
"Why? What crime has he committed?"
asked Pilate. But they shouted louder,
"Crucify him!"

When Pilate saw that he was getting nowhere, and that an uproar was starting, he took water and washed his hands in front of the crowd. "I am innocent of this man's blood," he said.

Then Pilate
released Barabbas.
He had Jesus flogged,
and handed him
over to be crucified.

Peter Disowns Jesus

Mark 14; Luke 22

Peter followed Jesus into the courtyard
of the high priest. He sat with the guards at the fire.

A servant girl saw Peter there in the firelight.
She looked closely at him and said,
"You were with Jesus."
But he denied it. "I don't know him," he said.

A little later someone else saw Peter and said, "This fellow was with Jesus."
Again Peter denied it.

After a little while, those standing near said to Peter, "Surely you are one of his disciples."

Peter replied,
"I don't know what
you're talking about!"
Just as he was speaking
the rooster crowed.

Jesus turned and looked straight at Peter. Then Peter remembered the words Jesus had spoken: "Before the rooster crows twice, you will disown me three times." And Peter broke down and wept.

Jesus Dies on the Cross

Matthew 27; Luke 23; John 19

Jesus carried his own cross to Golgotha.
There the soldiers crucified him.

Jesus said, "Father, forgive them, for they don't know what they're doing." A written notice above him read: This is Jesus, the King of the Jews. Two robbers were crucified with him, one on his right and one on his left. For three hours darkness came over all the land. And Jesus cried out in a loud voice, "My God, my God, why have you forsaken me?" Later when Jesus had cried out again, he bowed his head and died.

Jesus Is Buried

Matthew 27

As evening approached, a rich man named Joseph
went to Pilate and asked for Jesus' body.
Pilate ordered that it be given to him.
Joseph took the body, wrapped it in a clean
linen cloth, and placed it in his own new tomb.

He rolled a big stone in front of the entrance to the tomb and went away.
Later Pilate put a guard outside the tomb.

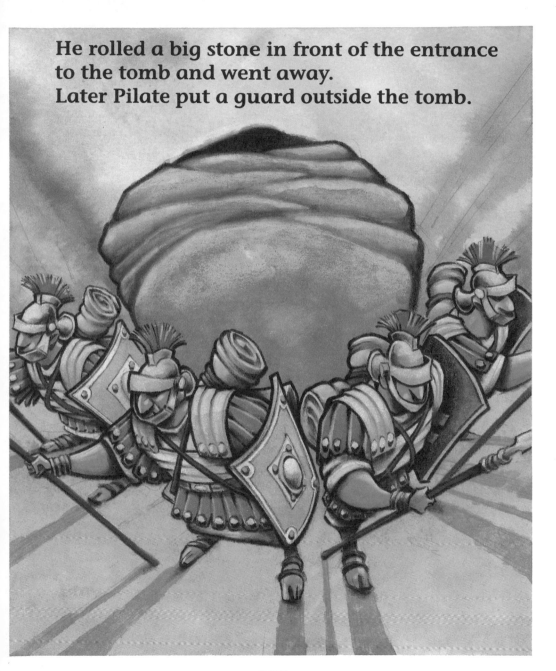

The Empty Tomb

Matthew 28; Mark 16; John 20

Early on the first day of the week,
while it was still dark, Mary Magdalene
and the other Mary went to the tomb.
They found the stone rolled away from the
entrance. As they entered the tomb,
they saw an angel dressed in a white robe.

The women were afraid.
"Don't be afraid," the angel said.
"You are looking for Jesus.
He is not here. He has risen, just as he said.
Go, tell his disciples and Peter."
The women hurried away from the tomb.
They were afraid yet filled with joy,
and they ran to tell the disciples.

Jesus Appears to His Disciples

Luke 24; John 20

On the evening of the first day of the week,
the disciples were together.
They had the doors locked for fear of the Jews.
Jesus came and stood among them and said,
"Peace be with you!"

After he said this, he showed them
his hands and feet and side.
The disciples were overjoyed when they saw Jesus.
Jesus asked them, "Do you have anything
here to eat?" So they gave him a piece of fish.
Jesus took the fish and ate it.

Jesus Goes Up Into Heaven

Acts 1

After Jesus appeared to his disciples
over a period of 40 days, he was taken up
into heaven right before their eyes.
A cloud hid him from their sight.

The disciples were looking up into the sky,
when suddenly two men dressed
in white stood beside them.
"Why do you stand here looking into the sky?"
they asked. "This same Jesus,
who has been taken from you into heaven,
will come back again."
Then the disciples returned to Jerusalem.

The Day of Pentecost

Acts 2

When the day of
Pentecost came,
the disciples were
all together.
Suddenly a sound
like the blowing
of a violent wind
came from heaven.
It filled the whole
house where
they were sitting.

Tongues of fire came to rest on each of them.
They were filled with the Holy Spirit
and began to speak in other tongues.

A crowd came together because each one
heard the disciples speaking his own language.
Amazed, they asked, "What does this mean?"
Some, however, made fun of the disciples
and said, "They have had too much wine."
Then Peter stood up and addressed the crowd:
"God has raised Jesus to life, and we are
witnesses of the fact. Repent and be baptized."
About 3,000 accepted his message
and were baptized that day.

Peter Heals a Beggar

Acts 3

One day Peter and John were
going up to the temple.
A man crippled from birth was being carried
to the temple gate called Beautiful.
He was put there every day to beg.

When the man saw Peter and John,
he asked them for money.
Peter looked straight at him, as did John.
Then Peter said, "Look at us!
Silver or gold I do not have.
But what I have I give you.
In the name of Jesus Christ, walk."
Taking him by the right hand,
Peter helped the man up.

Instantly the man's feet and ankles became strong.
He jumped to his feet and began to walk.
Then he went with Peter and John
into the temple courts, walking and jumping,
and praising God.

Philip and the Ethiopian

Acts 8

An angel of God said to Philip,
"Go south to the desert road
that goes down from
Jerusalem to Gaza."

On his way Philip met an Ethiopian.
He was an important official in charge
of all the money of the queen of the Ethiopians.
This man had gone to Jerusalem to worship.
On his way home, he was sitting in his chariot
reading the book of Isaiah.

Philip heard the man reading. "Do you understand
what you are reading?" Philip asked.
"How can I," the Ethiopian said,
"unless someone explains it to me?"
So he invited Philip to sit with him.
Then Philip told him the good news about Jesus.

As they travelled along the road,
they came to some water and the Ethiopian said,
"Look, here's some water.
Why shouldn't I be baptized?"
Then Philip and the Ethiopian went down
into the water and Philip baptized him.

Saul Becomes a Believer

Acts 9

Saul was a Jewish leader.
He was searching for those who believed
in Jesus in order to have them put in jail.

As Saul travelled to Damascus, suddenly
a light from heaven flashed around him.
He fell to the ground and heard a voice say to him,
"Saul, Saul, why do you persecute me?"
"Who are you, Lord?" Saul asked.

"I am Jesus, whom you are persecuting,"
the voice replied. "Now get up and go into the city.
You will be told what you must do."
The men with Saul stood there speechless.
They heard the sound but did not see anyone.

Saul got up from the ground, but when
he opened his eyes he could not see.
So the men led him by the hand into Damascus.
For three days Saul was blind.

In Damascus there was a disciple named Ananias. The Lord called to him in a vision, "Ananias! Go to the house of Judas on Straight Street. Ask for a man named Saul."

Then Ananias went to the house. Placing his hands on Saul, he said, "Brother Saul, Jesus who appeared to you has sent me so that you may see again and be filled with the Holy Spirit."

Immediately, something like scales fell from Saul's eyes, and he could see again. He got up and was baptized.

Saul in Damascus

Acts 9

Saul spent several days
with the disciples
in Damascus.
He began to preach that
Jesus is the Son of God.
All who heard him were
astonished and asked,
"Isn't he the man
who caused trouble
for the believers
in Jerusalem?"
After many days, the
Jews planned to kill Saul,
but he learned of their plan.
Day and night the
Jews kept close watch
on the city gates
in order to kill him.

But Saul's followers took him by night
and lowered him in a basket
through an opening in the city wall.

Paul and Silas in Prison

Acts 13; 16

While Saul, who was also called Paul, and
Silas were preaching in Philippi,
a crowd attacked them.
Paul and Silas were thrown into prison, and
the jailer was commanded to guard them carefully.

He put them in the inner cell
and fastened their feet in the stocks.
About midnight Paul and Silas
were praying and singing hymns to God.
The other prisoners were listening to them.

Suddenly there was a violent earthquake.
The foundations of the prison were shaken.
All the prison doors flew open,
and everybody's chains came loose.

The jailer woke up.
When he saw the prison doors open,
he was about to kill himself because
he thought the prisoners had escaped.
But Paul shouted, "Don't harm yourself!
We are all here!"

The jailer rushed in and fell
trembling before Paul and Silas.
He brought them out of prison and asked,
"Sirs, what must I do to be saved?"
They replied, "Believe in the Lord Jesus,
and you will be saved—you and your household."

Immediately he and all his family were baptized.
The jailer brought Paul and Silas
into his house and set a meal before them.
He was filled with joy because
he had come to believe in God.

Paul's Shipwreck

Acts 27

Paul and some other prisoners were
put on a ship to sail to Rome.
Before very long, the ship was caught by
a storm and could not head into the wind.

The men passed ropes under
the ship to hold it together.
Afraid that they would run
aground on sandbars,
they lowered the sea anchor and
let the wind drive the ship along.

On the fourteenth night the ship
was still being driven by the wind.
The sailors sensed they were approaching land.
Fearing that the ship would crash against the rocks,
they dropped four anchors and prayed for daylight.

Just before dawn Paul urged them all to eat.
"For the last fourteen days," he said,
"you haven't eaten anything. Now take some food.
You need it to survive. Not one of you will lose
a single hair from your head."
They were all encouraged and ate some food.

When daylight came, the sailors saw a sandy beach.
They decided to run the ship aground.
But the ship struck a sandbar and would not move.

Those who could swim were ordered
to jump overboard and get to land.
The rest were to get there on pieces of the ship.
In this way everyone reached land safely.

Jesus Is Coming

Revelation 21–22

I heard a loud voice saying,
"Now God is with men,
and he will live with them.
They will be his people,
and God himself
will be with them
and be their God.

He will wipe every tear from their eyes.
There will be no more death or crying or pain."

And Jesus said, "Behold, I am coming soon!
Blessed is he who keeps the words in this book.
Behold, I am coming soon!
I am the First and the Last,
the Beginning and the End.
Yes, I am coming soon!"

Index

If you want to read about a particular Bible person or event or about a lesson to be learned, use this list to find the appropriate story.

Words You Should Know

If you are unsure of the meaning of a word used in this book, look it up here.

A

Adultery—To be sexually unfaithful to one's husband or wife.

Advance—To go forward.

Anchor—Something heavy, tied to a rope, which is attached to a boat. When an anchor is thrown into the water, it keeps the boat from floating away.

Angel—One of God's heavenly helpers who brings messages to people.

Anoint—To pour oil on a person's head to show that he or she is chosen by God for a special purpose.

Ark—A huge, wooden boat with a flat bottom.

B

Baal—A pretend god that ancient people worshipped instead of the Lord.

Baggage—Suitcases.

Banquet—A big party with lots of food and lots of people, sometimes held to celebrate a birthday or a wedding.

Baptize—To sprinkle or pour water over a person, or to dunk a person in water, in order to show that his or her sins have been forgiven.

Basin—A bowl.

Betray—To turn a friend over to his or her enemies.

Birthright—The family blessing, power and possessions that the oldest son receives when his father dies.

Bitter—Not easy to accept, difficult, painful.

Blessing—God's favour, God's OK.

Bridegroom—A man who is getting married.

Bronze—A type of metal that is rusty-brown in colour.

C

Caesar—The Roman emperor or king.

Caravan—A long line of moving things, such as trucks or camels.

Census—A count of how many people live in a city, state or country.

Chariot—A fancy cart with two large wheels pulled by horses.

Crucify—To put someone to death by nailing or tying them to a cross.

D

Decree—An order that the king has made.

Debt—Money owed to someone.

Desert—Very dry and dusty land.

Despise—To hate something so much that you don't want to see it or be around it.

E

Elders—Older men who were the leaders in a city or community

Entertain—To make people laugh or to keep them busy having fun.

Estate—All the belongings of a person who has died, to be shared by family members who are still living.

Explore—To go on a trip to find new things or to search out new areas.

F

Famine—A time when there is not enough food to eat or water to drink.

Flogged—To be beaten on the back with a big whip.

Foundation—The solid bottom of a building that holds it up and keeps it from falling over.

G

Generation—The lifetime of a person; your grandparents, your parents and you are three different generations in one family.

Gnats—Small black flies.

Golgotha—The place where Jesus was crucified.

Governor—The leader of a state or country.

Gracious—Kind and loving.

Grain—Small hard seeds grown by farmers and usually used to make breads and cereals.

Grudge—Not willing to forgive someone for something they did to hurt you.

H

Hail—Pieces of ice that fall like rain. Hail can sometimes be as big as golf balls.

Hallowed—Holy, sacred.

Hebrew—Another name for an Israelite.

Herald—An official messenger of the king.

Holy Spirit—The third person of the Trinity. Jesus promised to send the Holy Spirit so that you would never be alone.

Hosanna—A Hebrew word of praise.

I

Idol—A statue made of wood or stone that is worshipped instead of the true God.

Image— A statue of a person or animal, sometimes used as an idol.

Incense—Spices that give a sweet smell when they are burned.

J

Jealous—To be angry or upset because someone else has what you want.

L

Language—The words that people in different countries speak. For example French people speak in French, Spanish people speak in Spanish, the British speak English.

Leprosy—A disease that causes sores on a person's skin.

Levite—A member of the tribe of Levi, the third son of Jacob and Leah. They were priests, and they took care of the temple.

Locusts—Grasshoppers.

Loom—A machine for making cloth out of thread.

Lyre—A stringed musical instrument.

M

Magi—The three kings who came to see Jesus.

Miracle—Something that doesn't happen naturally, that a person cannot do by his or her own power, such as making a blind man see or making a crippled man walk.

Misery—Feeling really bad about something.

Mock—To make fun of someone.

Mourn—To be sad.

Murder—To kill someone.

Myrhh—Very sweet perfume.

N

Nation—Many people living in one country.

O

Offering—A gift that you give to God to show thanks for what he has done for you.

P

Passover—A special holiday that the Jews have in springtime to celebrate when God freed them from slavery in Egypt.

Pentecost—The birthday of the Christian church, when the Holy Spirit came as promised by Jesus.

Persecute—To pick on or be mean to someone.

Pharaoh—The king of Egypt. He lived in a beautiful palace, and he had many slaves to take care of him.

Pillars—Tall round pieces of wood or metal that hold up a roof.

Plagues—Ten diseases and punishments that God sent to Pharaoh and the Egyptians because they would not free the Israelites.

Possessions—Things that belong to you.

Priest—A religious leader.

Property—Land that someone owns.

Prophet—A person who can tell what is going to happen in the future.

Q

Quail—A small bird that people ate as food.

R

Rabbi—A teacher.

Ram—A male sheep, usually with big horns.

Refrain—To stop or quit doing.

Reign—To rule over a country.

Repent—To say you are sorry for something you've done wrong.

Righteousness—To be right with God.

Register—To sign up for something.

S

Sacrifice—To give up something that is very special to you.

Samaritan—People who lived near the Jews and whom the Jews looked down on.

Sanctuary—A place for worship.

Sandbar—Hills of sand under water in a lake or ocean. Sometimes boats get caught on sandbars and cannot move.

Servant—Someone who is paid to do chores around the house for you or to cook for you.

Sheaves—Bundles of grain.

Stature—How tall you are.

Stocks—Wooden blocks with holes in which a prisoner's hands and feet could be locked in order to keep him or her from running away.

Stubborn—To want only your own way and what everyone else wants doesn't matter to you at all.

Survived—Lived.

T

Temptation—To want to do something that you know is wrong.

Tribes—Families who are related because they have the same grandparents.

Threat—Promised punishment or warning to force someone into doing something he or she doesn't want to do.

Tomb—A place where a person is put after he or she dies.

V

Virgin—A woman who has never had sexual relations with a man.

W

Wisdom—Understanding.

Widow—A woman whose husband has died.

Worship—To love and praise God.